SPRINGTIME FOR SNOWFLAKES

"Social Justice" and Its Postmodern Parentage

SPRINGTIME

FOR

SNOWFLAKES

"Social Justice" and Its Postmodern Parentage

a memoir by

MICHAEL RECTENWALD

Published by New English Review Press
a subsidiary of World Encounter Institute
PO Box 158397
Nashville, Tennessee 37215
&
27 Old Gloucester Street
London, England, WC1N 3AX

Cover Art and Design by Kendra Mallock

ISBN: 978-1-943003-18-1

First Edition

NEW ENGLISH REVIEW PRESS
newenglishreview.org

CONTENTS

PREFACE

AT THE MOMENT postmodern theory lay dying in the academy, it bore a child, namely, "social justice." As mothers are the root of all evil in horror films, so postmodern theory would be in waking nightmares. In horror fiction and conscious deliria, bad mothering means that blood will be spilled, usually by the child whose mind the mother has twisted into a pretzel. Like the Greek mythological characters Nyx and Echidna – who afflicted the world with such sinister offspring as Sleep, Death, Strife and Pain, Chimera, the Hydra, the Sphinx, and the Hesperian Dragon – postmodern theory also expelled its fearsome progeny. Social justice gestated within the university as postmodern theory ruled the roost. It was nursed during the Occupy movement and the Obama era. The financial crisis left its hapless followers in search of empowerment. It took root on the Internet in social media. But because its parent had taught it that the object world is not real, or else that the world at large was beyond one's purview, the child of postmodern theory could only change itself, as well as, so it imagined, those who bore signs of its oppressors. Although political correctness has enjoyed a much longer sway over academia, social justice as such debuted in higher education in the fall of 2016 – when it emerged in full regalia and occupied campuses to avenge its monster-mother's death and wreak havoc upon its enemies.

The phrase "social justice" recalls movements of the recent past that used the same political terminology. The civil rights movement comes to mind. But it would be a mistake to equate the contemporary social justice movement with this or other forerunners. Contemporary social justice embodies postmodern theoretical notions as well as the latter's adoption of Maoist and Stalinist disciplinary methods. And today's social justice creed is marked by preoccupations with new identities and their politics. It entails a broad palette of beliefs and practices, represented by new concerns and shibboleths, including "privilege," "white privilege," "privilege-checking," "self-criticism" or "autocritique," "cultural appropriation," "intersectionality," "discursive violence," "rape culture," "microaggressions," "mansplaining," and many others. The terms proliferate almost as rapidly as the gender identities.

Self-criticism and privilege-checking are the vestiges of "autocritique" and "struggle sessions," purification methods of the Cultural Revolution (1966-76). In the late 1960s, as word from the communist revival spread to the West through the student and feminist movements of Europe, especially France, the birthplace of postmodern theory, they became part of the Western left's vocabulary and toolkit. In struggle sessions, the guilty party – accused of selfishness, ignorance, and the embrace of bourgeois ideology – was pilloried with verbal and often physical assaults by her comrades, until she broke down and confessed her characterological and ideological flaws. Today, the confessions involve privilege, or the unearned advantage enjoyed by members of a dominant group based on appearance. Usually on demand, checking one's privilege means to acknowledge unearned advantage and to atone for it publicly. Meanwhile, in the Cultural Revolution, autocritique began with the guilty party, who subjected herself to brutal verbal self-inspection and denigration before the jury of her comrades. Autocritique and struggle sessions could lead to imprisonment or death as the comrade was often found to be insufficiently pure. In self-criticism (self-crit) and "callout" routines, soft forms of autocritique and struggle sessions became prevalent on the Internet sometime after 2009. They then infiltrated universities and other social spaces.

"Cultural appropriation" is the social justice version of the trespassing condemned in the Ten Commandments. The term refers to the adoption of elements of a subordinate culture by members of another, usually dominant culture. Accusations of cultural appropriation are legion. Several recent cases involve chefs and restaurant owners accused of wrongfully appropriating cuisine and restaurant themes. A notable instance involved the white Pittsburgh restauranteur, Adam Kucenic. Kucenic announced plans to open a "90s hip-hop themed fried chicken" restaurant – "The Coop" – in the predominantly black and gentrifying neighborhood of East Liberty. After the inevitable backlash, the entrepreneur turned to "The Good People's Group," a company that specializes in social justice self-awareness for white business owners. "The Good

People" apparently kick up social justice dust for such new business prospects – until they turn to "The Good People" for social justice consciousness-raising or "wokeness." Social justice is thus a new industry and a new business model.

On college campuses, social justice is evident with the prevalence of "safe spaces," "trigger warnings," "bias reporting hotlines," and the "no-platforming" of speakers – to say nothing of speech codes, the use of which in public institutions arguably abridges First Amendment rights.

In *Mapping Gay L.A.*, Moira Kenney traced the concept of "safe spaces" to gay and lesbian bars of the 1960s in Los Angeles and elsewhere, from which it made its way into feminist circles. As such, they became spaces free of men and "patriarchal" thought and expression. In colleges and universities, safe spaces are areas set aside for victims of unpleasant speech acts or "discursive violence." I have argued that in the context of higher education, safe spaces constitute a means of self-imposed cultural containment, not unlike that decried by Ralph Ellison, writing in reply to the socialist critic, Irving Howe, whom, he wrote, sought to consign him to a corked "jug" of cultural isolation not unlike that of the Jim Crow south.

Safe spaces were especially prominent after the election of Donald Trump as U.S. President. As college and university administrators went into crisis mode, they sought to provide students with spaces to relieve their post-electoral anxiety and distress. Safe spaces have been supplied with coloring books, crayons, therapy pets, and even pacifiers. They have come to most resemble hospital pediatric units.

Originating in feminist social media sites and blogs, the trigger warning (TW) migrated to the academy, where it became expected on syllabi for alerting students about course content that may be distressful, or "triggering" of negative emotions. Not only do trigger warnings curtail expression, they represent a slippery slope. As in the case at the University of London involving the first erotic novel written in English, *Fanny Hill, or Memoirs of a Woman of Pleasure*, the trend can lead to the removal of offensive texts from the curriculum entirely.

Bias reporting hotlines are means for students and others to contact bias administrators or "bias response teams" (BRTs) when they experience or witness a "bias incident," "bias infraction," or "micro-aggression." A bias incident, bias infraction, or micro-aggression is an event that results from biases toward members of marginalized groups, including races, sexual orientations, genders, or "non-gendered" people, and so on. Microaggressions or bias infractions may be reported to

BRTs, which generally act behind closed doors without transparency. On the website of my university (New York University) at least, I have been unable to find definitions of "bias incident," "micro-aggression," or even "bias." Yet the bias hotline is advertised and promoted widely on campus and online. Although the University of Chicago does not abide safe spaces or trigger warnings, like over 230 other colleges and universities nationwide, it has a bias reporting hotline.

Finally, no-platforming is the blocking of "dangerous" speakers from speaking on campuses, especially those expected to commit "discursive violence." The alt-right necessarily commits discursive violence. But many other speakers do too. Well-known *a priori* perpetrators include Milo Yiannopoulos, "alt-lite" provocateur and former technology editor at *Breitbart News*; Charles Murray, the political scientist and co-author of the controversial *The Bell Curve* (1994); conservative speaker Ben Shapiro, a YouTube personality who challenges transgenderism and other sacred cows of the left; and Dave Rubin, a classical John Stuart Mill liberal and host of popular YouTube talk show "The Rubin Report." Even classical liberals and idiosyncratic feminists like Christina Hoff Sommers and Camille Paglia are treated as discursive criminals.

The liberal response to objectionable speech traditionally had been to counter it with "more" and "better" speech. But the social justice left does not accept common notions of speech or expression. Social justice leftists have adopted from Critical Theory, liberal philosophy, and post-modern theory notions at odds with the U.S. Constitution. In his essay "Repressive Tolerance" (1965), the Frankfurt School critical theorist Herbert Marcuse (discussed in Chapter 5) argued that some expression is so intolerant of others as to be completely intolerable. Some speech and expression must be stopped and the left is correct and even obliged to stop it. "Pure tolerance" is impossible in liberal society. In *The Open Society and Its Enemies* (1945), the philosopher of science and liberal democracy Karl Popper was first to introduce this "paradox of tolerance" – a tolerant society requires a dose of intolerance.

The contemporary social justice creed also draws on "social and linguistic constructivism," an epistemological premise derived from postmodern theory holding that language constitutes social (and often all) reality, rather than merely attempting to represent it. Under social and linguistic constructivism, language is considered a material agent – its uses, as tantamount to physical acts. This belief explains the term "discursive violence." For the social justice believer, language can enact discursive violence by itself, without any attendant actions. Repressive tolerance, the paradox of tolerance, and social and linguistic constructivism make sense of the demands for no-platforming, trigger warnings, bias reporting hotlines, and safe spaces. As I will discuss below, social and linguistic constructivism is also the basis of transgender theory.

The U.S. Constitution protects distasteful speech, and at least thus far, the Supreme Court hasn't recognized the category of "hate speech." Yet social justice activists – including Antifa, the extracurricular social justice infantry – claim the role of *de facto* arbiters of speech and assembly. They make no bones about exercising their authority as such. As they see it, the First Amendment is flawed. They aim to fix the inadequacy. Social justice leftists apparently entertain no doubts about their qualifications for official arbiters of speech and other expression. One gets the feeling that they would sooner cut an opponent's tongue out than allow her to utter a single syllable with which they disagree. And given Antifa's credo, "by whatever means necessary," the feeling is not unreasonable. Social justice ideologues are authoritarian and anti-intellectual.

Intolerance and anti-intellectualism have become so commonplace on college campuses – with speakers routinely subjected to social justice sloganeering and chanting – that it came as little surprise to learn that Stanford University, placed fifth among national universities by *U.S. News and World Report* in its 2018 rankings, accepted undergraduate applicant, Ziad Ahmed. In response to an admissions essay prompt – "What matters to you, and why?" – Ahmed wrote "#BlackLivesMatter" one hundred times. Ahmed's acceptance, despite or because of his slogan-loaded "essay," is all the more remarkable because it came in 2017, a year in which Stanford accepted the fewest applicants in its history. Stanford culled its smallest-ever class from an applicant pool that university spokesman E. J. Miranda described as unusually rich with "intellectual strength and incredible diversity." In accepting Ahmed, Stanford essentially acknowledged – perhaps unwittingly, perhaps not – that the recitation of slogans plays an important role on college campuses today. Simply put, Stanford confessed that colleges and universities want singers in a social justice choir, students who demonstrate a willingness to swear allegiance to social justice, *ad nauseam.*

The anti-intellectualism and ideological straight-jacketing involved appears lost on administrators. And, it apparently poses no cause for concern for the vast majority of faculty. After all, since the social justice ideology is indubitably "correct," why not admit or even aggressively recruit perfervid social justice believers? Why not go further yet? Why not offer such promising disciples paying jobs as "Social Justice Peer Educators" (Washington State University), "Social Justice Advocates" (the University of Arizona), or "Diversity Peer Educators" (Harvard)? What could possibly go wrong?

Since I first took to Twitter as the @antipcnyuprof to issue jeremiads about and criticisms of social justice ideology, the absurdities and conflicts have only escalated. Tensions on campuses across the country have since involved social-justice-motivated protests, no-platforming, violence, and rioting. The newsworthy events at UC Berkeley, UC Santa Cruz, NYU, Middlebury, Evergreen State College, and elsewhere have proven that my earliest public pronouncements were not exaggerated, even though I intentionally employed the dramatic ruses of satire to emphasize the "problematic" issues.

By officially adopting and promoting the contemporary social justice creed, preferentially recruiting social justice novitiates and paying them to play active roles as part of an extended and extensive social justice administration, the institutions of North American higher education have taken a hairpin turn, and a wrong turn at that. They have surrendered moral and political authority to some of the most virulent, self-righteous, and authoritarian activists among the contemporary left. These activists have rallied other true believers, coaxed and cowed administrators, and corralled other, mostly quailing faculty, prompting them to applaud or quietly consent as the intellectual, cultural, and social cargo of millennia is jettisoned so that its freight can be driven "safely" through narrowing "tunnels of oppression." Having gone so far as to officially adopt a particularly censorious subset of contemporary leftist ideology, colleges and universities have tragically abdicated their roles as politically impartial and intellectually independent institutions for the advancement and transmission of knowledge and wisdom.

Academic freedom was sought by American faculty not so that they could endorse and justify received notions and dominant ideologies, but rather so that they and their students would be free to analyze and evaluate received notions and dominant ideologies against alternatives. As the American Association of University Professors stated in their 1915 "Declaration of Principles on Academic Freedom and Academic Tenure:" "Genuine boldness and thoroughness of inquiry, and freedom of speech, are scarcely reconcilable with the prescribed inculcation of a particular opinion upon a controverted question." Academic freedom means freedom from enforced adherence to a prescribed ideology. In mandating social justice ideology, universities have abandoned this legacy of open and free inquiry.

The derailment of academic institutions harms not only students but it also threatens the broader society, not only by undermining faith in knowledge claims but also by prejudicing the institutions supposed to cultivate the well-versed, thinking, and reasonable people required in a democratic society – people capable of open inquiry, debate, disagreement, and conflict resolution, without recourse to masks and knives.

How did this treacherous situation come to pass? How did the social justice creed gain dominance in academia? How and why was it made official policy in most colleges and universities in North America? Where did this social justice movement come from and how has it managed to permeate the broader culture and contend for domination?

To address these questions, we must look at the lineage of contemporary social justice. As I've said, social justice is the progeny of postmodern theory. Its beliefs, practices, values, and techniques bear the unmistakable birthmarks of postmodernism – although one must know what to look for. For this reason, and because social justice is having such a real-world impact, I call contemporary social justice "practical postmodernism," or "applied postmodern theory." These phrases should strike reasonable readers familiar with postmodernism as oxymoronic. How could such an obscure, anti-pragmatic, and nearly indescribable set of propositions as postmodern theory ever be applied or made practical?, they rightly ask. By being put into practice, I answer. Contemporary social justice is the very impractical "practical" application of postmodern theory to everyday life.

Understanding postmodern theory is indispensable for making sense of the contemporary social justice movement. But, as is well known among academics, extramural, non-professional criticism of "theory" is seldom well informed by what the theorists under attack have actually written.

In this volume, I treat postmodern theory and make sense of social justice ideology from an inside-out perspective – from the standpoint of an insider who is now an outsider looking back in. To draw a term from cultural anthropology, this treatment of postmodern theory comes from one who has long ago "gone native" and since returned. Unlike other accounts of postmodern theory, *Springtime for Snowflakes* is a first-person embodiment of the postmodern perspective, the result of a deep and extended immersion.

After recounting my kerfuffle with social justice ideology as a professor at NYU, I trace my induction into the postmodern, showing just how one becomes postmodern, and what the world looks like from within the postmodern point-of-view. Beginning with my high school and undergraduate educations, including a brief apprenticeship with the poet Allen Ginsberg, and continuing with my extensive graduate education in English and Literary and Cultural Studies/Theory, I aim to establish my academic and scholarly *bona fides* in leftist-dominated fields of study. This history makes my eventual renunciation of social justice, communism, and the political left in general all the more significant. I then turn to the problems posed by postmodern theory as I began to professionalize, to choose a particular theoretical perspective and object of study within the field of Literary and Cultural Theory/Studies and embark on a career. I trace my career path as I experienced difficulties with the increasingly nettlesome and fractious social justice creed, finally reaching the beginning of the story that follows. I end with a critique of social justice as the political expression of postmodern theory, a very brief discussion of social justice as a dominant ideology supporting corporate and "deep-state" interests, and finally a recommendation for an alternative creed.

CHAPTER 1
INTRODUCING THE @ANTIPCNYUPROF

O N SEPTEMBER 12, 2016, I established a Twitter account with the name "Deplorable NYU Prof" and the official handle @antipcnyuprof. This Twitter identity – replete with Friedrich Nietzsche avatar – represented a satirical character wielded by a self-proclaimed but anonymous NYU professor apparently gone rogue. As with all satire, the mockery was over-the-top, but the intended effect was serious criticism. The Twitter account allowed me to air views that I felt reluctant to issue under my real name, and to render them without undue circumspection.

As an NYU professor for nine years, I had grown concerned about recent developments within NYU and academia at large. With greater frequency, screeching mobs and the "no-platforming" of speakers essentially nullified freedom of speech. Speech codes and "bias reporting hotlines" curtailed the expression of entire communities. On matters of gender, sexuality, and identity broadly construed, whole avenues of inquiry were foreclosed on the basis of sacrosanct tenets deemed immune from scrutiny. Freedom of speech, academic freedom, and freedom of inquiry were under attack and in full retreat.

These assaults had been undertaken in the name of "social justice," a moral and political creed that had succeeded in gaining official acceptance within colleges and universities only two to three years earlier. Social justice debuted in higher education in the fall of 2016 – when it emerged to occupy campuses in order to avenge the death of its monster-mother, postmodern theory, and wreak havoc upon its enemies.

NYU's recent establishment of a bias reporting hotline, its cancellation of speakers based on political ideology, the talk of trigger warnings, and the growing use of safe spaces suggested to me that social justice had come home to roost in my university. I could no longer withhold my thoughts about the adoption of "social justice ideology" and "P.C. authoritarianism."

Deplorable NYU Prof
@antipcnyuprof

NYU professor exposes the viral identity politics of academia and its destruction of academic integrity.

New York, NY

nyu.edu/about/policies...

Joined September 2016

TWEETS	FOLLOWING	FOLLOWERS	LIKES	MOMENTS
90	666	693	130	1

Tweets   Tweets & replies   Media

Pinned Tweet

Deplorable NYU Prof @antipcnyuprof · Sep 12
Identity politics has, to borrow from Nietzsche, "made an infirmary of the whole world." @nyuniversity

Figure 1: Twitter profile of the DeplorableNYUProf (@antipcnyuprof)

Relishing the emancipation afforded by anonymity, I expressed views I knew to be quite controversial within academic circles. Here are but a few of the many tweets that I issued from the then anonymous @antipcnyuprof account:

• September 12: "Yes, contemporary identity politics on campuses today is integration in reverse!" (Linked to an article entitled, "California State Offers Segregated Housing for Black Students.")

• September 13: "The poor babies at Oberlin & Georgetown." (Linked to article entitled, "Christina Hoff Sommers Lecture Leads to 'Trigger warnings' and 'Safe Spaces' at Oberlin and Georgetown.")

• September 13: "I am trying, believe me, but under cover. Otherwise the PC Gestapo would ruin me." (Responding to a Twitter follower asking me to do something about runaway P.C. culture on campuses.)

• September 16: "I'm a NYU prof who's seen academe become a sham bc of identity pol & liberal totalitarianism. I'll tell all soon."

- September 27: "The 'academy' has officially gone ape shit. This is now merely mental illness posing as politics. #TriggerMyAss." (Linked to article entitled, "KU [University of Kansas] bars gorillas from jungle-theme decoration due to 'masculine image.'")

- September 29: "Liberalism coopts the discourse and techniques of radicalism and turns them into devices of mass manipulation."

- September 30: "I'll go Halloweening there as Nietzsche, who's been trigger-warned out of the curriculum, so no one will get it. What's yr costume idea?" (Linked to article entitled, "Penn State to costume-shame students with poster campaign.")

- October 11: "The identity politics left: they need a safe space that is at once a hall of mirrors and a rubber room." (Referring to both displays of narcissism by SJWs along with their demands for protection from "discursive violence.")

- October 22: "NYU: Milo Yiannopoulos Talk Canceled Due to 'Security Concerns' https://t.co/uNmUUYmJl4 (We don't want any snowflakes melting, now do we?"). (Linked to article entitled, "NYU: Milo Yiannopoulos Talk Canceled Due to Security Concerns.")

On October 11th 2016, I received a direct message on Twitter from the news editor for the Washington Square News, NYU's official student newspaper. The editor told me that a few of my tweets had somehow insinuated themselves into her Twitter alerts. She wanted to verify that I was actually an NYU professor, and if so, to know whether I might be interested in giving an interview. I agreed, not sure whether I'd go on the record under my real name.

I expanded liberally in response to her questions. After we finished, she asked me to pose for a photo. We had joked around a bit and she managed to snap a few shots that captured me laughing.

I spent a few hours pondering what I had said during the interview. I decided that my comments contained nothing remotely "deplorable." They merely presented an alternative viewpoint, one worthy of consideration. So, I agreed to let the paper run the piece, using my name.

Appearing in the Sunday print edition on October 23rd and followed by an online version on the next day, the interview was quite a shocker. Here was a full-time, long-term and non-tenure-track NYU faculty member protesting against "politically correct authoritarianism" and "social justice warrior ideology." While pointing readers to a hitherto anonymous Twitter account, the paper quoted my trenchant criticism of new NYU policies and trends in academia at large. I derided the adoption of safe spaces, trigger warnings, and the newly implemented bias reporting hotlines. I found this last contrivance, a recent addition to the arsenal of P.C. authoritarianism, especially pernicious. It turned everyone on campus into "sentinels of surveillance." I also panned the no-platforming of speakers by campus activists and their administrative enablers, as in the case of NYU's recent decision to cancel an appearance by right-wing Internet provocateur, Milo Yiannopoulos. The title of the interview undoubtedly colored its reading: "Q&A With a 'Deplorable' NYU Professor." The adjacent photo of me laughing added an additional layer of irreverence to my heresy.

WASHINGTON SQUARE NEWS

NYU's Independent Student Newspaper, est. 1973

f ⓨ ⓞ ⓝ   Search 🔍

NEWS ▾   FEATURES   ARTS   SPORTS   OPINION   MULTIMEDIA   SPECIAL EDITIONS   BLOGS   MORE

Q&A with a Deplorable NYU Professor

Diamond Naga Siu, **News Editor**
October 24, 2016

💬 f ⓨ ✉

Deplorable NYU Prof entered the Twitter-sphere with the handle @antipcnyuprof on Monday, Sept. 12. A real professor at NYU, he uses this account to argue against safe spaces, trigger warnings and the politically correct culture that imbues university settings.

His Twitter bio reads, "NYU professor exposes the viral identity politics of academia and its destruction of academic integrity."

Diamond Naga Siu

Michael Rectenwald, Liberal Studies clinical assistant professor, has been condemned and punished by members of the department for his controversial @antipcnyuprof twitter account.

ALLMODERN

WSN Newsletter

Get the day's top headlines delivered straight to your inbox!

Email address:

Your email address

Sign up

Figure 2 The opening salvo in my crusade against "social justice" ideology

I was officially outed.

To grasp the full implications of my gesture, one must consider not only the developments on college campuses, which would soon escalate, but also the wider political context. In just twelve days, after a circus campaign unlike any before, voters faced a choice. They would elect either Hillary Clinton or Donald Trump for President of the United States. Only ardent loyalists believed in Trump's chances. During the primary and final campaign, Trump swung wildly and indiscriminately at opponents. He was accused of stirring up every form of bigotry and reaction. And, political correctness numbered among his occasional targets. On September 8th 2016, Clinton referred to Trump supporters as "a basket of deplorables." Tens of thousands immediately adopted the designation as a badge of honor, incorporating "deplorable" into their Twitter names.

The publication of my interview set several proceedings in motion. Articles about the interview appeared in several venues, including *The Washington Times, Fox News, Campus Reform,* and *HeatStreet.*

What I didn't realize but would soon learn was that select NYU administrators and a small contingent of faculty had quickly formed a counter-insurgency and plotted a coordinated response that began to unfold within forty-eight hours of the publication of my interview.

CHAPTER 2

BECOMING DEPLORABLE

CALLED ON THE CARPET

ON OCTOBER 26, 2016, at 12:23 PM, near the tail end of a writing class that I was teaching in Silver Hall at New York University, I received a foreboding although not entirely unexpected message. The Dean of Liberal Studies and my direct supervisor, Fred Schwarzbach, sent me an email. It read as follows:

> Michael,
>
> I wonder if you could stop by my office at 2 today (which I think is between classes for you). I'd like to touch base about something that has just come up.
>
> Thanks …
> Fred

My class was scheduled to end at 12:30, but when the notification popped up on my laptop screen, I scanned the message and suddenly felt queasy. Distracted, I reminded the students of the upcoming readings and dismissed the class. Before leaving the room, I replied to the email:

> Hi Fred,
>
> I'm pretty sure I know what this is about. I will stop by.

M.

Of course, I agreed to "stop by." How could I not? Although I was somewhat disarmed by his casual reference to our pending confab, I had a strong presentiment about the intended topic of conversation. I packed my laptop and headed to my office to wait for the appointment.

Dean Schwarzbach invited me in and greeted me with a cautious smile. As we shook hands, he drew very near me, our faces no more than six inches apart, and whispered:

I want you to know that this meeting has nothing to do with your Twitter account or interview.

Oh, I answered, slightly relieved.

But something did not feel quite right. If the meeting had nothing to do with my Twitter account and recent interview, why then did he mention them in the first place? And why, as he only then announced, was the head of Human Resources, Shabana Master, to join our meeting – with my "permission?"

I hadn't noticed Ms. Master in the anteroom of the dean's office; she seemed to appear out of nowhere. Naturally, I agreed to have her join us. The three of us sat around the circular table in front of the dean's desk. He began somberly:

People are concerned about you.

Why? I asked.

He elaborated only a little, saying that more than one person among the staff or faculty had expressed genuine concern for my well-being. One such person had even pleaded with an unnamed administrator, contending that my interview and Twitter account signified "a cry for help." Although he tried to elude indelicacy, the dean was referring to supposed concern for my mental health.

Who said that? I asked.

I can't answer that question, he replied. Such matters are confidential. But more than one person has expressed concern.

More than one?

Yes.

Is this some sort of trick to push me out for my views?

Not at all, he gravely insisted.

Some ten minutes of conversation ensued. I remember little, other than the solicitude the two labored to convey, and the outcome they clearly wished to effect. My health and wellbeing were of paramount importance, they insisted, and everything else paled by comparison. I would begin a paid medical leave of absence, effective immediately. I would be relieved of my teaching and other duties, and my classes would be turned over to other instructors.

I realized that this suggestion represented a serious personal and professional affront, while at the same time presenting a perilous "choice." If I accepted the leave, I effectively admitted to the claim. On the other hand, as a non-tenure-track contract faculty member up for promotion, the administration held significant power over my career prospects. And two high-ranking administrators had made eminently clear a desideratum (originating from 'who knows where'), that I abide by their wishes and accept the leave. They obviously wanted me to absent myself from the university for a while. The crux was thus the length of the leave, and who controlled my return.

For how long? I asked.

For at least the remainder of the semester, the dean answered. You can come back next semester, or extend the leave, if necessary. It's up to you.

What about my students?

I asked, because as far as I knew, I was the only writing professor in the Liberal Studies program who taught first-year writing as an introduction to scholarly discourse. I believed strongly in my approach and had spent over four years developing a writing-across-the-curriculum textbook used throughout the U.S. and Canada. My worry was that after laying the groundwork for such scholarly writing, my classes would be redirected to focus on navel gazing, turning students to self-reflection without context. After I explained my concerns, I was promised that the replacement instructors would faithfully adhere to my syllabi.

They will teach your courses as you designed them, Ms. Master stated unequivocally (a promise that was not kept, as I later learned).

The sooner the transfer of the classes takes place, the better, the dean chimed in.

Are you sure I'm not being pushed out because of my recently published views? I asked again.

That was not the case, they both reassured me.

At the close of the meeting, the dean offered to have Ms. Master escort me to my office and to have her accompany me while I remained on campus. I noticed the averted gazes and disapproving glances of a few colleagues. I now had the distinct feeling of being treated like someone who had contracted an ill-defined and hideous disease. Ms. Master followed me to my office, shadowing me as if I posed a danger. She stayed for a painfully long time, until I suggested that she could go.

Coincidently, a reporter for the *New York Post* called soon after Shabana Master left. The reporter had seen my interview and subsequent developments and was following the story with keen interest. She said that she and others at the *Post* sympathized with my views and sided with me against the university's treatment.

I was befuddled by this mention of the university's treatment, given that she could hardly have known about my recent meeting and its outcome. I told her that I had just been placed on a paid medical leave of absence and that I wasn't entirely sure what to make of it.

The reporter was unambiguous in her response.

The timing of a paid leave of absence was very suspicious, she said. It was especially suspect in light of the recently published interview, and the open letter denouncing you.

What open letter?! I asked.

She informed me that an open letter had just appeared in the *Washington Square News*. In fact, she had called to see if I wanted to make a statement about it. It read as follows:

Letter to the Editor: Liberal Studies Rejects @antipcnyuprof's Faulty Claims, by Members of the Liberal Studies Diversity, Equity, and Inclusion Working Group

October 26, 2016

In "Q&A with Deplorable NYU Professor," Liberal Studies Clinical Assistant Professor Michael Rectenwald states the following in response to a request to talk about his thoughts on diversity: "A cis, white, straight male like myself is guilty of something. I don't know what. But I'm fucking sure I'm guilty of it. And I am very fucking low on the ethical totem pole, you know?" After reading the interview and Professor Rectenwald's @antipcnyuprof tweets, we would have to say we do know. We regretfully agree that Professor Rectenwald is guilty of something, though not by reason of his race, gender or sexuality. *And though we have never seen an "ethical totem pole," on the basis of his interview comments and tweets that denigrate NYU students, faculty and administrators, we imagine that Professor Rectenwald might be rather low on it.*

First, he indulges in *ad hominem* fallacies. He seeks to discredit many of us who are committed to social justice by calling us insane and suggesting that some of our concerns are crazy … Frankly, I'm not really anti-pc. My contention is that trigger warning, safe spaces and bias hotline reporting are not politically correct. They are insane."

"Identity politics on campus," he goes on to say, "have made an infirmary of the whole, damn campus. Let's face it: every room is like a hospital ward. What are we supposed to do? I can't deal with it—it's insane." And later still: "the crazier and crazier that this left gets, this version of the left, the more the more the alt-right is going to be laughing their asses off plus getting more pissed." Professor Rectenwald's rhetoric repeatedly suggests that mental illness invalidates the ideas and feelings of those who live with it. We categorically reject such rhetoric and its stigmatizing effects. *We reject, too, Professor Rectenwald's efforts to gaslight those who would disagree with him and to silence responses to his incendiary rhetoric by dismissing claims before they are reasonably made.* If Professor Rectenwald is not, as he notes in the interview, against diversity, then why doesn't he use language that substantiates his professed point of view? Diversity, in any case, is too often reduced to numbers — neither effective nor dynamic without strategies such as equity and inclusion, values Professor Rectenwald's language works against …

A quick glance at Professor Rectenwald's Twitter page shows not only further flaws in his thinking — circular arguments, appeals to consequences and hasty generalizations — but also statements that are callous at best. One of his tweets goes so far as to casually support students killing themselves in response to Donald Trump's rhetoric. Another warns of "explosive" proof that faculty colleagues are "frauds" who were hired on the basis of their identities rather than on the basis of their merit. We fully support Professor Rectenwald's right to speak his mind and we welcome civil discourse on the issues that concern him. But as long as he airs his views with so little appeal to evidence and civility, we must find him guilty of illogic and incivility in a community that predicates its work in great part on rational thought and the civil exchange of ideas. The cause of Professor Rectenwald's guilt is certainly not, in our view, his identity as a cis, white, straight male. *The cause of his guilt is the content and structure of his thinking.*

Signed by the following members of the Liberal Studies Diversity, Equity and Inclusion Working Group: … (emphasis mine).

Signed by two deans, four faculty members and four students, the letter was either a willful misreading, or an egregious misinterpretation of my Twitter account and interview remarks. It either indicated dishonesty or that the committee collectively exhibited subpar reading skills. The letter wrongly declared that I had engaged in *ad hominem* attacks, when in fact I never pointed to any individuals or mentioned any persons by name, least of all anyone in this working group. It falsely claimed that I had called members of this group or others insane. I had clearly pointed to cultural trends and used the word "crazy" not in any clinical sense or to refer to the mental health of any individuals. It wrongly claimed that I employed logical fallacies, although I did not commit any fallacies. (I tutored college logic by my second semester in college. It seemed that I had known more about logic at nineteen than these committee members did when they drafted this letter.) The letter endowed me with magical powers, like the ability to "gaslight" the committee members, suggesting that I had intentionally sought to do so with my remarks. Meanwhile, the committee had never crossed my mind, either while I posted tweets, or during my interview. I had forgotten that the group even existed. And gaslighting cannot be accomplished by the mere expression of opinions. The committee members clearly had no idea what gaslighting meant. The letter stated that I lacked evidence for my claims about the "social justice" excesses happening on college campuses, but the committee's ignorance of the constant stream of news of social justice outrages did not equal a lack of evidence on my part. It merely meant that they had no idea what was happening on campuses across North America – as reported regularly. The letter suggested that I "casually support students killing themselves in response to Donald Trump's rhetoric," but that tweet was clearly a joke, and when I made it I had roughly 500 followers, none of them NYU students. Students only became aware of the tweet after the committee pointed them to it.

I was now more inclined to give the reporter her story. So, I asked her again what she made of this series of events. She emphatically declared that there was no way that these three incidents – my interview, the open letter, and the strongly-suggested leave of absence – were unrelated. The leave was definitely punishment and I was being forced out of the classroom for my views. Period.

I decided to go on record. I talked about the Twitter account, the interview, the open letter, and the leave of absence.

The New York Post broke the story on October 30th: "Professor Who Tweeted Against PC Culture is Out at NYU." I didn't like the headline, because it implied that I had been fired. But sunlight was the best disinfectant, the reporter assured me. If she was right, I risked more by my silence than by full exposure, even if that exposure included a mis-leading headline.

The story went viral. At first, coverage came from the usual con-servative suspects – *The Washington Times, Fox News, Breitbart News,* and *The Daily Caller,* among others – who seized upon my case as fur-ther evidence of the leftwing dictatorship and P.C. policing in academia. But *The Washington Post, Inside Higher Ed, The Chronicle of Higher Education, Adweek, New York Magazine, Reason,* and many others fol-lowed suit. With a few exceptions, this first-round coverage defended me against the institutional goliath and its Orwellian tribunal. A few media outlets noted my earlier tweet expressing my apprehension that if I ever revealed my name, members of "the PC Gestapo would ruin me." Sure enough, a few articles suggested, they were trying to do just that.

Hours after I appeared on *Varney and Company,* a morning show that aired on Fox Business News, Dean Schwarzbach sent me a short, severe email, clearly in response to this appearance on major network TV. He stated that I had been dishonest in the media about the leave of absence; it was voluntary, not compulsory. He asked me: Do you still want this leave of absence?

Yes, I responded.

Then, after mounds of negative press, NYU's P.R. department struck back, using this email exchange against me. They took what I understood to be a private email exchange between the dean and myself and published it on the university website. They then apparently point-ed reporters to it. A few liberal outlets picked up the exchange, with one claiming that I was not only anti-P.C. but also "anti-truth." Again, technically, my medical leave was "voluntary." NYU could not legally force me to take a medical leave of absence. But, as I have suggested, the strong recommendations from two high-ranking NYU administrators that I take a leave seemed quite compelling. To put it mildly, my "choice" to accept their "offer" was significantly conditioned by the power differ-ential between them and me. Surely, the good liberals and leftists in the media and among the thousands of Internet assailants who trolled me understood that. Finally, I wrote Dean Schwarzbach that I still wanted the leave because by that time, over two weeks had already passed since I began the leave, my classes had already changed hands and the instruc-tors had not followed my syllabus as promised. The semester had gone too far downstream to turn back. I had no real choice but to stay out on leave. So, yes, I still "wanted" the leave, a leave that was not my idea at all but rather NYU's from the beginning.

AN INADVERTENT PROMOTION OF DIVERSITY

Then, on November 7, during my leave and just one day before the stunning election of Donald Trump, I received an email from the Dean of Arts and Sciences, announcing my promotion, retroactive to September 1st. I was promoted from Clinical Assistant Professor to (full) Clinical Professor, an advancement of two academic levels, hurdling over associate rank.

To most observers, my promotion signified nothing less than a complete reversal by NYU. Numerous media outlets positively described it as such. *The New York Post* declared, "New York University just struck a blow for diversity of thought on campus – by promoting Michael Rectenwald, who'd been put on leave after outing himself as the anti-PC tweeter, DeplorableNYUProfessor."

Being denied the promotion would have constituted gross discrimination. I will not detail my qualifications as compared to the other colleagues who had also applied for the same promotion and received it but suffice it to say that none had stronger academic credentials. While an external committee reviewed the applicants' dossiers and issued findings on their merits, their reports were only recommendations to the NYU decision-maker. That was the Dean of Arts and Sciences, Dean Schwarzbach's supervisor. He was undoubtedly quite familiar with my case when he officially authorized my promotion.

My successful bid for promotion should not be confused with a ringing endorsement of diversity of thought on campus, however. It did suggest that academic freedom and due process were more likely to prevail when external scrutiny and broader social pressure were brought to bear on academic institutions. If I had not gone on the record with the media, my promotion and career might have been buried alive.

"YOU MUST BE A RIGHTWING NUT-JOB"

My public criticisms of social justice ideology and politically correct authoritarianism resonated with large swaths of the political right. I gained a sizeable new audience and support network – through Twitter, Facebook and via hundreds of supportive emails. I also drew backing from "cultural libertarians," as Paul Joseph Watson dubbed this newly-emergent "counterculture." It should come as no surprise that many Trumpists backed me, especially given Trump's regular (although non-specific) criticisms of political correctness.

Criticism of political correctness was supposed to be the exclusive province of the rightwing. For most observers, it was almost inconceivable that an anti-P.C. critic could come from another political quarter. Unsurprisingly, then, the majority of people who discovered my case, including some reporters, simply assumed that I was a conservative. As one Twitter troll put it: "You're anti-P.C.? You must be a rightwing nutjob." But as I explained in numerous interviews and essays, I was not a Trump supporter; I was never a right-winger, or an alt-right-winger; I was never a conservative of any variety. Hell, I wasn't even a classical John Stuart Mill liberal.

In fact, for several years, I had identified as a left or libertarian communist. My politics were to the left (and considerably critical of the authoritarianism) of Bolshevism! I had published essays in socialist journals on several topics, including analyses of identity politics, intersectionality theory, political economy, and the prospects for socialism in the context of transhumanism. I became a well-respected Marxist thinker and essayist. I had flirted with a Trotskyist sect, and later became affiliated with a loosely organized left or libertarian communist group.

It wasn't only strangers who mistook me for rightwing or conservative. So too did many who knew better. An Anti-Trump mania and a reactionary fervor now gripped liberals and leftists of nearly all stripes. Previously unaffiliated and warring left and liberal factions consolidated and circled the wagons. Anyone who failed to signal complete fidelity to "the resistance" risked being savaged.

After my appearance on Fox Business News, such rabid ideologues ambushed me. The social-justice-sympathetic members of the left communist group to which I belonged denounced me in a series of group emails. Several members conducted a preposterous cyber show-trial, bringing charges against me and calling for votes on a number of alleged transgressions. From what I could tell, my worst offences included appearing on Fox News, sounding remotely like a member of an opposing political tribe, receiving positive coverage in right-leaning media, and criticizing leftist milieus just as Trump became President.

I denied that these self-appointed judges held any moral authority over me and declared their arbitrations null and void. Meanwhile, the elders of the group (one a supposed friend of mine) had remained silent, allowing the abuse to go on unabated for a day. When they finally chimed in, they called for my official expulsion. I told them not to bother as I wanted nothing further to do with them; I quit. In their collectivist zeal, they later stripped my name from three essays that I'd written for publication on their website and assigned their authorship to someone else entirely. Upon discovering this fraudulence, I publicly berated them for plagiarism. Aaron Barlow, a prominent member of the American Association of University Professors, noticed my complaint and investigated the alleged breach of intellectual integrity. Verifying my authorship of the essays, he condemned the group's actions in a popular blog. Only then did the benevolent dictators return my name to the essays' mastheads.

Friends and acquaintances from other communities also turned on me with a vengeance, joining in the groupthink repudiation. After my appearance on *The O'Reilly Factor* on Fox News, the Twitter attack was so fierce, vitriolic, and sustained that my associate Lori Price and I spent a whole night blocking and muting tweeters.

But the worst banishment came from the NYU Liberal Studies community – to which I had contributed a great deal, and of which I had striven for years to be a well-regarded member. Soon after the open letter appeared, I recognized a virtual universal shunning by my faculty colleagues. One after another, colleagues unfriended and blocked me on Facebook. The few that didn't simply avoided me entirely, until I saved them the trouble and unfriended them. Most stinging were the betrayals of those who once relied on my generosity, some whose careers I had supported and considerably advanced.

Despite the harsh treatment doled out to me by the social justice left and the warm reception I received from the right, I did not become a right-winger, or a conservative. But after the social-justice-infiltrated left showed me its gnarly fangs and drove me out, I could no longer identify as a leftist. Yet I also refused the libertarian label, even though the denotation of the term addressed many of my concerns.

Part of the problem was that our conventional political vocabulary had been adulterated beyond recognition – utterly ruined. In any case, I no longer felt at home in any political grouping. I could not adopt a label or declare an allegiance to a single political perspective without feeling that I thereby misrepresented my viewpoint and reality itself. What this made me was a specimen of a vastly outnumbered, widely dispersed, and still unchartered breed – a political animal with a (weakened) herding instinct, yet without a herd.

VINDICATED, PAINFULLY

The fallout from my Twitter prank and the backlash over subsequent media exposure proved the point of the entire exercise. As they responded to my criticisms, the social justice ideologues both inside and outside of the university demonstrated their authoritarian and fanatical character. With their notoriously vituperative, outrageous pack-and-attack mentality, they showed that they routinely victimize others, all the while playing the victim. They most closely resembled religious zealots. Like other types of religious zealots, they sanctioned no debate, recognized no counter-evidence, shut down free expression (of alternate views), foreclosed free inquiry, rejected reasoning, and brooked no questioning of their sacrosanct dicta.

Finally, in their response to my challenges to the social justice creed, NYU administrators effectively ceded control to the social justice ideologues in their midst, just as the administrators at Evergreen State College in Washington state would later do. They betrayed the fact that social justice ideology was now official doctrine in the university, just as I had suggested.

In the following pages, I return to the birthing room and primary incubator of the social justice creed: the field of English Studies. In the English department, we will find the theoretical, political, and ideological progenitors of the social justice creed. I will examine the field by peering through the lens of my own graduate education in English Literature, Literary and Cultural Theory, and Cultural Studies. But first I must explain just how it was that I came to study postmodern theory in the first place.

CHAPTER 3
PRE-POSTMODERN

AN INOCULATION

THERE WAS LIFE before postmodernism. Although not exactly like "Leave It to Beaver," it was simpler, more coherent, and ontologically more secure in terms of assumptions and identities. "Girls will be boys, and boys will be girls. /It's a mixed up, muddled up, shook up world, /Except for Lola. Lo lo lo lo Lola," the Kinks sang in 1970, when I was eleven. Except it wasn't so mixed up as such, not for me, and not for anyone I knew. And the Kinks made clear that the world wasn't so shook-up and mixed-up, simply because "Lola" could still be sung as such. Once the shakeup came, such lyrics would be deemed transphobic and bigoted beyond redemption, as the dustup about Lou Reed's "Walk on the Wild Side" (1972) recently demonstrated. That would change but not for what seemed like an eternity. But change would come, and I would eventually enter the postmodern vortex.

Viewed from a sociological standpoint, I was an unlikely candidate for the obscure, highly theoretical educational indoctrination into postmodern theory. A closer consideration of my personal history yields a different picture.

A few years ago, my brother Art, the youngest of my eight siblings and the owner of a national construction company, sent me a digital version of a photograph of Robert J. Rectenwald. Art keeps the photo on his desk to remind him of his background. Taken in the mid-to-late 1970s, the image pictured our dad in his early fifties, standing in the basement of our Waldorf Street home on Pittsburgh's North Side. Covered in soot, he looked at the camera defiantly, as if daring the picture-taker to a

31

challenge. I posted the image to Facebook, adding the caption: "Working-class history, mine." Leftist and Marxist friends rushed to congratulate me for being the son of a coal miner and a union man. But my father was not a coal miner; he was a home remodeler – an independent contractor, a Reagan Democrat, and never a fan of unions.

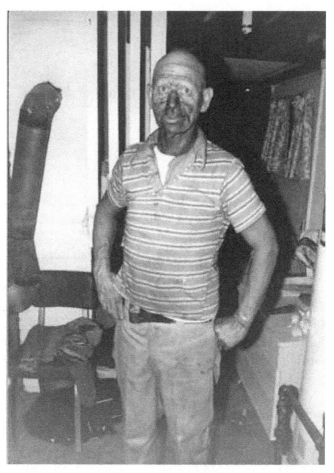

Figure 3: Robert J. Rectenwald, Home Remodeling Contractor, Pittsburgh, PA, circa 1975

Beginning in the late '60s, from age eight or so, when I walked alone at night, I noticed what seemed like an abnormal darkness about the air and sky. I wasn't sure whether the super-darkness had been augmented by my eyes and thus had come from my head, or whether the nights were in fact darker than normal. I was soon reassured; the added darkness was not an exaggeration of my fertile imagination. Pittsburgh harbored a dirty secret: accumulated soot from industrial exhaust permeated everything. The black dirt that covered my dad was not coal dust from a mine, but a by-product of the smoke-belching steel mills that lined the riverfronts. Gutting the original walls of houses released decades of particulates that had burrowed behind thick plaster.

Regularly practicing such mental exercises that tested my subjective impressions against a background of observations corroborated by others, I developed habits of mind that served as an inoculation that prevented me from ever going "full pomo," from leaping into the deep end of the postmodern abyss. Postmodern theorists and their followers have had a fondness for placing "the real" within ironic scare quotes. This pretension suggests that acknowledging an object world makes one naive. The snubbing of empirical information and the "innocent" flirtations with anti-objectivity have more often than not amounted to sheer nonsense. More importantly, such feigned bracketing of "the real" betrays the experience of those who wrestle with matter to stay alive – namely, everyone.

From age nine or so, I was expected to work for the family business – on Saturdays during the school year, and on any given summer weekday. I carried tools and lighter building materials upstairs into strangers' cramped bathrooms, then sat vacantly on the toolbox as dad worked and swore at walls that were never square. I was responsible for handing him the proper tools upon request, like a nurse assisting a surgeon.

In our home on Waldorf Street, "Waldorf Hysteria," as we dubbed it, we enjoyed whatever wealth we had in part by comparison. For example, as a home-owning family, we knew that we were better off than the lower-working-class tenants of Bonvue, a street parallel to ours but lower in elevation by half of a football field and half of a socioeconomic class. The two streets were linked by Zolium, a steep, hard-edged, uneven cobblestone city bypass seldom traveled by cars. But the rapid acceleration on bike or sled down Zolium Street clued us in to the possibility that we could fall any day, bouncing along the uneven cobblestones as we tumbled down. Overhearing my parents' conversations, I learned to worry about economic decline and even collapse. My anxiety increased when, as I opened the refrigerator door between meals, my mother pleaded, "Please go easy!"

One summer, when I was thirteen, my dad landed a big job – replacing the flooring and cove base in the student dining halls of Carnegie Mellon University. My assignment was to use a hammer and chisel to remove the old cove base that clung stubbornly to the corners of the walls and floors. During lunch break one day, my dad remarked on the good job I'd been doing. He then gazed out into the quadrangle, at once peering across the campus and into the future. He told me that given my intelligence and work ethic, I could very well attend such a university as this. I knew his statement was a compliment but also that it conveyed a duty. As far as I knew, although I was the seventh of nine children, I was the first (and last) to receive this particular kind of encouragement from our dad. As it happened, I would in fact earn my Ph.D. from this very university.

When the time came to choose a high school, my father suggested that I apply to Shadyside Academy, the city's best prep school. As Dad and I sat in the office of the headmaster after touring the campus, I sensed an obstacle, and one emerged. The headmaster explained, "Mr. Rectenwald, although I believe your son would do well here academically, I'm afraid that he wouldn't fit in … socially. It's a social class issue." At least that's what I remember about that very deflating encounter. This experience and others like it increased the chances that if ever exposed to it, I would seriously entertain Marxism. I had gotten several tastes of classism and had begun to develop class resentment.

But for now, I was a devout Catholic. Catholicism became meaningful to me after receiving the sacrament of confirmation in the sixth grade. I remember leaning over the kitchen counter during the lunch celebration following the ceremony. As I cut a piece of cheese from the block, a sense of my own maturation came over me. I felt that I'd become an adult, a person of conscience. I hadn't at all expected such sentiments to emerge, but they did.

"MY WAY"

Partly because I had become an earnest Catholic but mostly because I wanted the best education I could get regardless of the personal cost, I attended St. Fidelis Seminary High School, a Catholic boarding seminary attached to a Capuchin monastery. The school resembled the prep school that turned me away, except that the regimen was much more severe. It included religious training. Weekends home were rare. We followed a rigid daily schedule. And, we renounced all contact with members of the opposite sex – or "girls," as they were called in the early 1970s. Our daily schedule was set in stone: early morning prayer, mass, classes (even on Saturday mornings), two and half hours of daily silent study hall (with two on Sundays), evening prayer, and nine nighttime hours of compulsory silence. I took pride in my capacity to endure the inflexible schedule, the lack of home comforts, the limited familial contact, the rural isolation, the depravation of other-sex contact, and the intense pain of loneliness and longing. But two years was all I could take. By spring of sophomore year, when I showed my spiritual advisor love poems I'd written for Carol Sajko, a girl back home, I had already decided to leave.

Back from the seminary for my junior and senior high school years, I began to battle with my dad. He expected me to play football for Pittsburgh North Catholic, my new school. Despite special pleading from him and my mom – Please do it for him! she implored – I refused. Instead, a stab in his back, I became the team cameraman and filmed the games.

Being an intellectually-inclined working-class kid involved two obstacles. You had to justify yourself both inside and outside the family. Willingness to take on this double jeopardy explains the lengths to which I was willing to go to become an academic – even before I entered graduate school. I asserted and defended intellectual pursuits for their own sake. I tried to convince my parents, especially my dad, that a literary or intellectual vocation, whatever it meant career-wise, had real, immeasurable value. My mother was clearly sympathetic but said little. Once, I went so far as to read them the final few sentences of Percy Shelley's *A Defence of Poetry* (written 1821, published 1840), which ends: "Poets are the unacknowledged legislators of the world." I delivered the last line as if I'd just reached the summit of Mont Blanc. But my "drop-the-mic" moment represented mere histrionics to my dad.

"*Unacknowledged* is right!" he quipped. He was smart, and had no use for a litterateur, least of all one among his own brood. As I learned, he especially had no patience for *poetry* – whether it was Carl Sandberg's muscular industrial paeans or Shelley's Promethean triumphalism made not the slightest difference. One evening, while watching TV, I disparaged Paul Anka's "My Way" (sung by Jim Neighbors on *Gomer Pyle*) as romantically individualistic. He responded bitterly: "You're very good with words, aren't you?" The implication was that words alone were insufficient, not that they weren't important. After all, he had just delighted in the song's lyrics. His remark stands out now as an apt criticism of postmodern theory itself: you're good with words, aren't you?

I decided to study pre-med at Allegheny College in Meadville, Pennsylvania. I did very well, but I harbored a secret wish to study literature. I fancied myself a budding poet and read and wrote poetry every night after I finished studying chemistry, biology, and math. In the spring semester of my sophomore year, I took a second English course beyond the required 101. "The Experience of Poetry" was taught by Professor Alfred Kern, a novelist from Alliance, Ohio. As the title suggested, the course was an experiential study. A soulful and emotional man, Alfred Kern encouraged us to relish poetry rather than merely analyzing it. Kern was particularly fond of Keats, Wordsworth, and other Romantics. Students were also encouraged to write and develop their own poetry and to participate in a student reading at the end of the semester.

On January 29th that year, Terri Dodds, a classmate and friend who knew of my mostly secret penchant for writing poetry, had given me a birthday present. Tearing off the wrapping paper, my eyes lit on a pocket-sized booklet with a black-and-white cover. A sloppy print job endowed the book with a sense of its having been stolen onto the press in the middle of the night, collated and glued to the cover in the morning, and sold for five dollars to hungover bohemians by afternoon. The logo of the publisher, City Lights Books, a "Y" with a ball for a head between two arms, reminded me of the robes of the Capuchin friars. *Howl and Other Poems,* by Allen Ginsberg, Introduction by William Carlos Williams (1955) seemed off-center on the cover and title page. I had read some William Carlos Williams, but not his protégé.

The poems were raw and deliberately messy, yawning across and filling the entire page. Like the physical book itself, they had a disjointed and stitched-together feel, which vouched for their authenticity. "Howl" struck me as powerful and brilliant, yet crazy, or quite close to it, as if tempting the reader to join in the howling it described. I devoured it and the poems hidden behind this baldly heretical spiritual testament – "A Supermarket in California," "Sunflower Sutra," "America," and the others. While similarly quixotic, these seemed less tormented, and funnier than the title poem. In all, I was struck by the embrace of the personal and social at one and the same time. Allen Ginsberg seemed to take in everything, without exception. And he had a voice, a way to articulate mad ideas, longings, quests, failures, and love. I bought all the Ginsberg books I could afford, including his newly-released *Journals –Early Fifties Early Sixties* (1978). I tried to the follow the reading diet he had laid out for himself in the notebooks. His prescriptions took me to the early nineteenth-century mystic, William Blake; to *A Dark Night of the Soul,* by St. John of the Cross; and to the post-surrealist and mushroom-tripping French madman, Antonin Artaud, among others. Ginsberg and his whole literary tribe challenged the implicit or explicit philosophical materialism of my biology and chemistry professors, while suggesting that a reconciliation of personal, political, and social reality was possible.

To supplement the class, Kern brought three major contemporary poets to campus for poetry readings. The one I remember, Robert Pinsky, read from his book *Sadness and Happiness* (1976). Having read Ginsberg's wild verse made such "academic" poetry seem utterly timid and tame, like it was wrapped in gauze. I didn't understand why it clung so closely and exclusively to the intimate and private. During the recitation of one piece, a young woman, possibly a student but not one from class, shrieked, heaved, then cried convulsively. I had no idea why. I hadn't heard anything disturbing. The trauma was entirely interior and struck me as utterly inappropriate. Looking back, her outburst preluded the social justice ideologues, especially on Trump's inauguration day. Yet like the rest of Pinsky's poems, this one merely made me feel claustrophobic; if anything, I wanted to yawn.

During the last two or three classes, we read our own poetry. I had written a few poems in which I tried to straddle the breach between what I took to be the hyperbole of intimacy in the poetry that Kern and most of my peers seemed to prefer, and the tossed salad of Ginsberg. I didn't want to read or write political manifestos, but neither did I want to dwell exclusively on the big toe of my father.

That summer, I decided to change majors – to English. Stunned and alarmed, my father warned me: you are making a grave mistake. Then I doubled-down, suggesting that I might venture to the Jack Kerouac School of Disembodied Poetics at Naropa Institute in Boulder, Colorado – to study poetry with Allen Ginsberg. My dad was utterly flummoxed. I'd learned from my friend Rich Lamping, a philosophy student at Notre Dame, that Ginsberg was teaching at Naropa and taking on an apprentice. I wrote to Ginsberg to apply, enclosing a small batch of poems. I was thrilled when I received a response. On a postcard – scribbled in the typical Ginsbergese, rife with ampersands and dashes – Ginsberg wrote that I had "natural rhythm" and "an uncanny intelligence in language," ending with "so sure, come here to study." I'd gotten the apprenticeship.

Until the last minute, my dad hoped and begged me to come to my senses and return to Allegheny in the fall. But I didn't. I stayed home and took a job at a fast-food restaurant to save money for the spring. By November, I had enrolled at Naropa and bought my bus ticket from Pittsburgh to Denver. After what proved an emotionally tumultuous fall, during which time I suffered from a depressive episode and panic attacks, the time came to embark on my odyssey – to become an apprentice to the most unabashed poet-celebrity in America. As I loaded my trunk into the truck-bed of loyal friend and apprentice plumber Mark Robinson, my stoical German-American dad wept openly in the driveway.

CHAPTER 4

"THE GLORIOUS MYSTIC FROM PITTSBURGH"

"NO PLANT THAT GROWS ON MORTAL SOIL"

AFTER A THREE-DAY Greyhound bus trip from Pittsburgh to Denver, capped by a final hour-and-a-half leg from Denver to Boulder, a grueling and psychologically torturous trip had finally ended. As the bus had pulled through terminal after terminal in innumerable dreary towns and cities across the Midwest, I felt like I was trapped inside a crumby literary sequel, a stale continuation of *On the Road*, or some other disjointed, sojourning prose.

I was met at the Boulder bus station by a pony-tailed cowboy in his late thirties, apparently a hanger-on at Naropa assigned to pick me up. Preoccupied, he spoke nary a word, clearly deeming me and the cross-country marathon that wrung me out as thoroughly unremarkable. As I would learn weeks later, the quiet ride was provided courtesy of Dick Gallop, poet and friend of Ted Berrigan, with whom I took a class at the Jack Kerouac School of Disembodied Poetics. Gallop dropped me off unceremoniously at Naropa, which was located in a retail space in an outdoor mall on Pearl Street.

I hadn't yet arranged for a place to live and had nowhere else to go, so I waited inside the school, thinking I'd eventually run into Ginsberg. I was exhausted, disoriented, and feeling appropriately disembodied. The school struck me as very weird. This feeling would epitomize my experience there. I was afraid of the strangeness in the New Ageist, Eastern-spiritual, patchouli-scented, Carlos-Castaneda-mountain-peak-hopping, mushroom-tripping, floatation-tank-filled Boulder and its Naropa epicenter. So, I clung to Ginsberg, who at least seemed familiar, and regularly ate matzo ball soup in the nearby New York Deli. That Allen Ginsberg was perhaps the least bizarre person around should tell you much about Naropa Institute.

After hours sitting on my trunk outside the library, Ginsberg finally showed up. His first spoken words to me were yelled: "What are you doing?! Have you read Mayakovski yet?! Have you read Neruda?! I'm editing a volume of long-verse poetry! What long-verse poetry have you read, other than mine?!"

He was alarmed that I had been sitting outside of the library, rather than riffling through its books of poetry inside. When I didn't answer, Allen's fury was quelled just as quickly it had flared up and he switched to an exaggerated gentleness. He decided that I should leave my trunk in the library, while we walked to his apartment.

During that first night with Ginsberg, I felt as if I had awakened to a dream to which I'd suddenly become accustomed, a feeling that came to characterize most of my experience of him. On the way to his apartment on Mapleton Street, several blocks from the school, Allen discussed poetic ambition and fame: "Fame is not really real," he said, a statement that he would echo many times. "Nobody is real except the people we're close to." He cited a passage from Milton's lyric poem, "Lycidas":

"Fame ... that last infirmity of noble mind ... no plant that grows on mortal soil." Who did Allen refer to with this allusion, I wondered – himself, me, both of us, or everyone who ever wrote poetry?

He wondered how I could afford to study with him and why I had taken such a dramatic step, which he knew had involved leaving a pre-med track after two successful years, to become the apprentice of an aging Beat poet. I had received grants from the government, I answered, which seemed to surprise or even disappoint him. Was he now that acceptable to the feds? As for why I'd come, I reminded him of the two letters I'd sent him, in which I'd already explained myself, and to which he'd replied with encouragement, including an offer to become his apprentice.

Although in his fifties, Allen Ginsberg apparently hadn't tired of bohemian asceticism. His apartment was Spartan. Naked blond hardwood floors; a kitchen floor and walls lined with black-and-white tiles; a dining room containing a galley table and two folding chairs, where Allen and Peter Orlofsky ate meals and Allen's typewriter was placed; a living room with nothing but a piano and stool for furniture; and two bedrooms, each with nothing but a mattress and meditation pillow on the floor. The whole place appeared not to contain a single knickknack, decoration, painting, or other artwork – not even a houseplant.

By the time I left Allen and his apartment, it was night. The stars illuminated the pastel adobe houses scattered across the Boulder mesa, which seemed to float beneath the westward mountain peaks and somehow reminded me of a desert and an ocean floor at once. I headed back to the college to check the bulletin board and find temporary encampment. I found a spot at a house where six or seven new Naropa students and a few fellow travelers lined the walls of the basement with makeshift beds comprised of sleeping bags and blankets. I stayed there for a few days, until three of us decided to rent a small bungalow on Marine Street – but not before we took mescaline together. I had a nine-hour trip during which I imagined I was trapped inside the belly of the beast of William Blake's poem "The Tyger." Walking around Boulder on mescaline, I was tormented with a sense that I was in the inferno. Had I somehow traveled into hell, and if so, why?

A SEASON IN HELL

After this early hellish vision, the next several months were some of the most interesting and instructive of all my life. As an apprentice and teaching assistant to Ginsberg, I commanded large blocks of his time, as he did of mine. I typed his poems while he looked over my shoulder and screamed if I made the lines break where I thought they should, rather than at the end of the page. I helped with the editing of the long-verse poetry anthology that included Mayakovski and Neruda among many others. And we discussed my poems. It was a classical mentor-student relationship, with time devoted to discourse on any and all matters – political, religious, philosophic, literary, practical – interspersed with downright arguments.

Allen read my poetry carefully, providing feedback and advice. Among the dozens of books that he recommended, Allen gave me a few and even inscribed two to me. One was his New Directions copy of Arthur Rimbaud's *A Season in Hell*. He knew that I had been having my own season in hell and that he was a major character in it. Looking back, it was not a bad plot-line for my unconscious to have conjured. If a young poetic hopeful was going to have a hell experience, one could think of few better or more literary ways to undergo it than with one of the most famous American poets alive, one best known for his hellish visions. Allen was my Virgil, accompanying me on my personal sojourn into the Inferno.

Yet, in true Blakean dialectical fashion, my time with Allen was also a marriage of heaven and hell. I had my share of epiphanies. Once, while Allen sang Blake's Songs of Innocence in his Basic Poetics class, I fell into a trance and had a vision of the Lamb of God weaving a web of sleep around the heads of little children. I talked and wrote about this, causing some alarm in Allen and my advisor. However, I proved that I wasn't crazy. What I had experienced was purely affective and not at all psychotic. Given my religious background and propensities, Allen inscribed his copy of the *Poems of Gerard Manley Hopkins* and gave it to me.

Of course, being around Allen Ginsberg meant endless phone calls, visitors, and heaps of mail. I remember opening a scathing letter from City Lights publisher and anarchist poet Lawrence Ferlinghetti, who wrote bitterly about Bob Dylan's then new album, "Slow Train Comin'" (which I loved). "I don't have to serve anybody!" Ferlinghetti ranted to Allen about Dylan's song, "Gotta Serve Somebody" – as if he was blaming Allen for Dylan's recent conversion to evangelical Christianity.

In addition to such curious scenarios, Allen's public persona had also become an unmanageable Frankenstein monster. I noticed with no little anxiety the responsibility he felt to legatees of the Beat Generation, those who'd gambled to become Beat authors but hadn't succeeded, like he had. He was tormented by drunken beatnik wannabes arriving at his front door at all hours of the day and night, wondering what, if anything, he owed them.

William Seward Burroughs III, better known as William S. Burroughs Jr. or simply as Billy Burroughs, was undoubtedly the most conspicuous casualty of the Beat generation. In fact, Burroughs's life may be one of the most tragic in contemporary literary lore. Despite being born into the Burroughs office machine dynasty and living periods of his childhood among a West Palm Beach elite that included the Posts of breakfast cereal notoriety, Billy's life was striking for the horrific childhood experienced at the hands of his father, the famous Beat novelist, William Burroughs II. (Billy and a later co-author scrupulously chronicled the nightmare of his life in his brutally forthright, posthumously-published autobiography/biography, *Cursed from Birth: The Short, Unhappy Life of William S. Burroughs, Jr.*)

In early May, after I'd spent over four months as his apprentice, Allen departed for a poetry reading tour that included stops in India and China. He left me to house-sit his apartment and care-take of Billy, who had come to town just before Allen left. Allen made clear that I should expect difficulties.

As he swilled six packs of Colt Malt Liquor and mumbled curses and incoherencies to himself, Billy manifested a serious disturbance. Sporting a formal top hat, carrying a cane, and exhibiting a bulging forehead, he reminded me of Edgar Allen Poe, appearing misplaced in the late twentieth century. When I escorted Billy to Tom's bar to buy more malt liquor, his paranoia was palpable. His sudden and frequent about-faces to see who was following him, his eyes popping like hard-boiled eggs, made him appear an utter madman.

On that first night together, I listened to Billy as he told me how he'd been traumatized, when, at age four, he watched as his father fatally shot his mother in the head during a game of William Tell gone bad. The sin of the father was later revisited upon the son. He told me how, while living with his grandparents in West Palm Beach, at fifteen, he accidentally shot a friend in the neck. Although his friend survived, Billy described his emotional response, which sounded like a nervous breakdown. He recalled how he then descended into heavy drug use, which would eventually lead to cirrhosis of the liver, kidney disease, and mental illness.

Billy told me that his father had advised him that if he hoped to become a great writer, he needed to undergo "extreme experience," as if he hadn't already. Taking drugs, William S. Burroughs II suggested, was the best shortcut. Since the father had already exhausted heroin and Ginsberg had fairly well explored LSD, speed was one of the few remaining options. Billy told me that his father essentially advised him to become an amphetamine addict.

At night, Billy read from his Bible and ranted under his breath. He was evidently seeking salvation of some sort. Finally, he told me that he just wanted to die. He read a suicide note he'd written, which I have in my possession to this day.

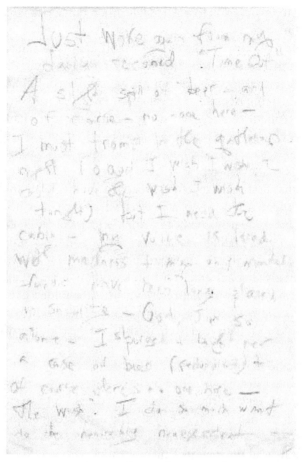

Figure 4 Suicide Note from Billy Burroughs, May 1980

The tortured lines read as follows:

Just woke from my daily _____ 'Time Out' A slight spill of beer—
and of course—no one here—I must tromp the gathering night (o
god I wish I wish, I could have the wish I wish tonight) but I need
the cabin—My voiced is laced with madness & my only mental
funds have long been placed in security—God, I'm so alone—I
splurged and bought a case of beer (redundant) & of course there's
no one here—The wish? I do so much want to be honorably nonex-
istent.

Billy fled to Florida and died that summer of cirrhosis, at age 33.
His ashes were brought back to the Rockies.

THE MIND'S OWN PROCESSES

At the end of the semester and my apprenticeship, with other student poets, I read some of my poetry at the Naropa spring arts festival poetry reading. I read only poems I had written during my short time at Naropa. Allen introduced me as "the glorious mystic from Pittsburgh" and referred to me as "the mad mystic from Pittsburgh" after I'd finished reading – apt appellations, I think, as I read poems that bore a clear relationship to the Christian mystic tradition, especially the poetry of Gerard Manley Hopkins. But the influence of Ginsberg was also apparent.

Allen Ginsberg was, of course, a signal participant in several of the counter-cultural movements of the fifties and sixties that contributed to postmodernism, which emerged by the late sixties. As I would later write in a conference paper from my graduate school years entitled, "Radical Niche Marketing: Allen Ginsberg, Postmodernism, The Body and the Media" (1996): "If the anti-modernist, counter-cultural movements, of which Ginsberg was a prominent figure, were incubators of postmodernism, then perhaps we will find the postmodern taking shape in such a figure." I argued then, years after I'd studied with him, and maintain now, that Ginsberg did prefigure postmodernism, if not contributing to it directly. The eclecticism of his poetry, its inclusion of everything that crossed his mind, the juxtaposition of low and high culture and the metaphysical and the mundane, its eventual shift in emphasis from transcendence to immanence, its rejection of both capitalism and communism, its investment in the body as the final seat of morality and politics, are among the features that marked him as a postmodern forerunner.

Yet, I also noted that his poetry and politics had roots in a much older, liberal humanist tradition that stems back to the Protestant Reformation: "Ginsberg's insistence on the political sanctity and inviolate right to the expression of the mind's own processes is akin to Milton's belief in the right to personal conscience with reference to the Bible, of freedom from censorship..." Indeed, despite his postmodernist tendencies, were he alive today, I believe that Ginsberg would be utterly appalled by and severely critical of the social justice left's authoritarian character – its censorious, censoring, and prohibitionist proclivities.

CHAPTER 5
THE SEDUCTION OF THEORY

ONE DIMENSIONAL MAN?

HAD MY DAD understood it, my graduate school enrollment in "Literary and Cultural Theory" would have struck him as tantamount to madness, like self-commitment to an insane asylum. After the Ginsberg apprenticeship, which definitively ended any remaining prospects I had for medical school, he wouldn't have had tears left to cry. Perhaps that partly explains why I got married, had three children, and worked in advertising for nine years first, waiting until my early thirties to begin grad school. By then, my father had been considerably reduced, physically and cognitively, by a series of strokes. I no longer had to answer to him, even if I wanted to.

So, twelve years after the Ginsberg apprenticeship and after working in broadcast advertising for nine years, by my early thirties, I finally decided to become a literature professor. I sought what Freud suggested was an indispensable element for approaching fulfillment – "meaningful work." The main requirement for meaningful work as I saw it was intellectual autonomy, the freedom and independence to think, write, explore, and teach what I came to know. In advertising, I was using my talent, at least to some degree. I almost believed that I had found a fulfilling career. But by age thirty-one, I thought that I was wasting my life. My days were spent in offices, conference rooms, and restaurants, talking about story boards, ad campaigns, network buys, rating points, demographics, psychographics – and I came to care less and less about it all. Often feeling disembodied, I hoped that strangers would not look at me in my suit and tie as I walked along the sidewalk. What they saw

46

was not really me.

When I wasn't at work, after time spent with my wife Gretchen, and the kids, I read incessantly, often into the dawn. I read far more than I had in college. There is nothing better than a crisis (or prohibition) to provoke an ardent quest for knowledge, or more like it, answers. My reading was not merely a matter of curiosity but primarily a desperate attempt to understand my predicament. I paged through Daniel J. Levinson's *The Seasons of a Man's Life* (1978) and concluded that I had taken a faulty first career path. I read Carl Jung's discussion of the torpor that one endures while gestating a new life phase, which explained my lack of enthusiasm for anything other than reading and writing. I came across a reprint of a 1984 Harper's Magazine article entitled, "Big Brother Is You, Watching," an analysis of media that articulated much of what I had sensed about TV – that it ironized, ridiculed, and eroded individuality by virtue of appealing to the exclusive existence of a non-descript and self-effacing mass selfhood. The essay referred to the Frankfurt School of Critical Theory, particularly Theodor Adorno and Herbert Marcuse. I would discover, only after knowing him for several years, that my friend and NYU colleague Mark Crispin Miller was the author of "Big Brother is You, Watching."

Then, in a bookstore of a Bethesda (Maryland) mall, I chanced upon the unlikely shelving of a striking title: *One Dimensional Man* (1964). It entranced me. Herbert Marcuse argued that both capitalist and communist societies were totalitarian. Barely touching on the Eastern bloc, however, he directed his scathing critique almost exclusively at the West and the U.S. in particular. The "technological rationality" of "administered life" in "advanced industrial society" infiltrates existence and effectively mass-produces and controls everything. In meeting needs and even in providing affluence for some, it eradicates individuality. The system determines needs and then satisfies them, making for a "willing" conformity with its own demands. The administered society is "totalizing" – nothing, not even criticism of it, escapes its reach. I thought of my hero, Bob Dylan; he refused the role of political spokesman, writing sometimes bizarre, surrealistic, reflective, and lovelorn songs instead. But by Marcuse's reckoning, even, or especially, the caustic criticism of his early folk career had been commodified and coopted.

My discovery of *One Dimensional Man* came just as I had risen in the field of broadcast advertising. After four years of scrounging for a living at local radio stations and advertising agencies in Pittsburgh, by twenty-eight, I was finally doing well. In D.C., where John-Michael,

Gretchen and I had moved, we introduced two more children to the family of three: Molly and Dylan. We lived comfortably in a posh Bethesda condominium complex. Yet *One Dimensional Man*, and moreover, my alienation, made me feel that my enjoyment of relative material affluence had come at the cost of my true self. Looking back, I see a penchant for self-sabotage, a determination to look for and find whatever might undermine any success I could enjoy. I wonder whether this tendency was the result of some recessive leftist meme that had infected me. Or, was something really wrong with the culture that set me on the path to discover what it was? Was my ennui the cause of my quest, or was the quest the cause of my ennui?

I spent considerable time writing poetry and short fiction. I needed seclusion, so I established writing spaces everywhere we lived as I was transferred from Pittsburgh, to D.C, to San Francisco. I established a child-resistant bunker in the closet of the condo in Bethesda. After transferring to San Francisco, I hung drywall in the garage of our stucco-covered bungalow in Kensington, CA, then spent untold hours thrashing out poetry and short fiction. I submitted batches of poetry to small literary magazines, mostly with the expected result: "We're sorry, but…" Finally, "The Eros of the Baby Boom Eras," a short poem about my daughter Molly, caught the attention of a poetry magazine, *The New York Quarterly*, edited by William Packard. Ginsberg had recommended the magazine to me a few years before. My poem ran in an issue along with poetry by Charles Bukowski, a coup that compensated for all my expenditures in ribbons, typing paper, envelopes, stamps, time, the hope that preceded dejection, and dejection itself.

The more earnestly I pursued my literary avocation, the more estranged from my money-making career I became. I was plagued with thoughts that my life was being wasted and that I should become something more. Perhaps I'd been possessed by a ridiculous romanticism, "foundationed deep somehow," as Bob Dylan put it in the song, "My Back Pages." In any case, I was driven to distraction – until I submitted.

The story of my postmodern education begins with a successful escape – from the "prison house" (Frederic Jameson) of corporate America – where I had been consigned for nine years – and into what I took for the last remaining haven of intellectual independence – academia. I would learn much later that academia demands as much if not more conformity than any other corporate field. In fact, the conformity penetrates much more deeply. You not only have to buy into the ideology, you must rehearse and recapitulate it without fail. Otherwise, you are deemed politically regressive. You might even be a "Nazi."

I went ahead, leaving a relatively high-income position to under-take what some told me was not only impossible but possibly insane. I had a few friends in the know. They repeated the well-worn truisms. "There are no jobs in academia." "As a white male, your chances of getting a job in the humanities are quite remote." "You can't raise three children, do full-time graduate work, teach at least one class per semester (required for the tuition remission and stipend), and hold down yet another job, all at the same time." These warnings did not dissuade me. In fact, remarkably, they strengthened my resolve. Gretchen went along with it and picked up some of the slack money-wise by eventually returning to her career in property management.

However, the career path I'd chosen involved transformations of a wholly different kind than these. The sharp reduction in income, the many nights of curtailed sleep, the sacrifice of almost all other forms of "entertainment," the stress and strain on family and marriage, and the certain prospect of uncertain prospects: these were only the preconditions of the story, not the story itself.

An incident in the summer before I was slated to begin the M.A. in English at Case Western Reserve University provided a hint that I had little to no idea of what I was getting into. I had been showing our townhouse in Pittsburgh for rent. We were set to move to Erie, PA, where I'd found a job running the advertising department of a radio station of the Erie branch of Penn State University, from where I'd commute to classes at Case Western in Cleveland. One rental prospect was a 25-year-old woman – let's call her Evita (I don't remember her actual name). While showing Evita around, I asked, "So, what brings you to Pittsburgh?" She said that she was beginning grad school at the University of Pittsburgh (Pitt), in … English. Of course, I couldn't let the coincidence pass without remark. I told Evita of my plans. We both appreciated the serendipity.

Yet, as we discussed the field, Evita uttered a phrase – "Cultural Studies" – which was foreign to my ears. As I would soon learn, Cultural Studies wasn't exactly what it reminded me of – cultural anthropology. As its founders Stuart Hall, Raymond Williams and E.P. Thompson suggested, Cultural Studies was invented to be a politically radical engagement with culture, especially "low" forms, including mass media and other popular culture. Hall, Williams, and Thompson were Marxists. They saw culture as a form of power and a carrier of capitalist ideology. Combined with Antonio Gramsci's ideas about "cultural hegemony," Cultural Studies, and not the Frankfurt School, is the real source of anything like "Cultural Marxism," the menace decried by many on the right. Cultural Studies accounts for a good share of your "radicals in the academy."

Evita mentioned her plan to focus on "cultural objects" from early twentieth-century African-American culture, although she was unsure exactly which ones, or what "theoretical paradigm" she would work under. I didn't quite register "theoretical paradigm." I had some understanding of the meaning, but apparently a different one from hers. As an undergraduate in English at Pitt, where I finished my B.A., I had taken a course in the Philosophy of Science. The course grappled with methodologies and the nature of science, and with various epistemological theories. Thomas Kuhn's *The Structure of Scientific Revolutions* (1961) impressed me as the most ground-breaking at the time. Kuhn described major revolutions in science in terms of "paradigm shifts," akin to gestalt shifts in individual perception and cognition, and similarly resulting in major changes in emphasis and self-understanding. (I was about to undergo one myself.) Kuhn's work impacted Science Studies, the theoretical field I later chose. By suggesting that science responded to shifts in convention, authority, and social beliefs, Kuhn seemed to leave the door open for sociologists and others, who saw in his work a confession of sorts, an admission that science could be impacted by cultural and social forces, which sociologists could study, and thereby explain the very content of scientific knowledge in terms of social factors. Meanwhile, Kuhn disavowed such interpretations and said he was a fairly strict "internalist." He saw science as driven by its own impetus and internal logic, and not by such external factors as ideology or social interests.

I said that I hadn't heard of Cultural Studies, emphasizing the phrase with a slight dismissal.

Evita answered, "Well, we'll see who does better on the market in the end – the English literature traditionalist, or the Cultural Studies maven."

To my then-retrograde ears, this sounded like vulgarity uttered in church. I hadn't even considered the notion of a market in literary academia, let alone types of scholars and scholarship competing in a market. I wanted to get away from markets! Little did I know, although the field never ceases to criticize the capitalist marketplace and the commodification of the worker and culture, English Studies is no less commodified than any other profession. In fact, the attention and consideration required to "package," "brand" and "re-brand" the scholar and her work is as thoroughgoing if not more so than anything I'd done as a pitchman for consumer brands.

Evita delivered her market statement with a conceit, suggesting that these two "types" represented antagonists, and that she held a particular dislike for one of them, the one I apparently favored. But I didn't favor anything. I simply didn't know about the division she referred to. She implied that a struggle between an old and new guard was afoot. Apparently, the field of English had changed since I left college in the early 1980s. Our respective positions, although mine was merely reflexive, had already made us opponents. I resented that she somehow saw me as politically regressive based on an apparent preference for literature over anthropology or sociology. I decided that renting to her might be a mistake but I let her decide. She didn't take the place.

A PEPPY NIHILISM

In mid-August, I met with my adviser, Professor Roger Salomon. An early septuagenarian, Professor Salomon matched most peoples' image of an English professor: tweed blazer with elbow patches over a wool sweater, thick-wale corduroy pants. He offered me a chair, not across from his desk, but beside his own. I sensed the spiritual community that abided in his office, an ongoing séance between himself and the living, breathing books – a communication with great authors, who were supposedly dead. Salomon recommended that I start by taking only one course per semester for the first year. He felt confident that I might be very interested in a course called "Cultural Criticism," taught by Professor Martha Woodmansee. He read the course description aloud, which included the neologism "McDonaldization." The syllabus seemed to smirk with a sense of subversive glee at the prospect of roasting the field itself, with an attitude that might be described as a peppy nihilism. This was certainly not a path that Roger Salomon had taken or would ever have taken. The syllabus mocked the very values that he held dear. He knew that once put on the path trodden by Martha Woodmansee, I might never turn back. Yet noble soul that he was, he passed the torch, and me with it, to Martha Woodmansee.

I tried to get a grip on Woodmansee before the start of the semester. A little research made clear that she was obviously a sage academic, not only *au courant* in the field but also steeped in European cultural history and philosophy. She had Master's and Doctoral degrees in both

German and English from Stanford. She knew Kant, Hegel, Marx, and the notorious Frankfurt School – in the original German and in English translation. The precise name for her own approach is called new historicism. New historicism is a method marked by attention to "historicity," or the specificity of historical moments and events, as opposed to universal verities. New historicism holds that our only access to the past is through "texts," broadly construed as any carrier of signification or meaning-making. But contrary to an "old historicism" as it were, texts don't exist in a vacuum handed down to us through literary history but rather in conversation with other texts, including "non-literary" texts – all of which are involved in ongoing discourses. Texts are not mere reflections of the past but interventions into ongoing conversations of their era – rhetorical structures that have to be read closely in order to discern and then excavate their meaning and import in connection with the conversations within which they intervened.

In extreme forms, historicism, old or new, can veer toward an environmental determinism that portrays human beings as hapless objects of circumstance. As for the "genius" of a "great writer," like Herman Melville for example, it could be cultivated on an ordinary tomato plant, given the right soil and other environmental conditions.

Martha, as she encouraged us to call her, took a liking to me, and vice versa. On the first day, just after I introduced myself to the class, Martha declared, "the very smartest English graduates go into advertising, not academia." This came off as a compliment but also suggested that I must have caught a sudden case of stupid. Martha made clear that she considered her colleagues hopelessly passé and fetishistic in their obsessive focus on "authors." She said mockingly that the real action had lay in "'cultural problems,' not in literature."

"Cultural Criticism" was a primer in Theory and Cultural Studies. It started with the Frankfurt School, the group of German Jewish intellectuals who founded the Frankfurt Institute for Social Research at Frankfurt University in 1923, then fled Nazi Germany in 1933. Max Horkheimer, Theodor Adorno, and Herbert Marcuse emigrated to the United States and took refuge at Columbia University and later at U.C. Berkeley and elsewhere. Their writing inaugurated two fields of study – Critical Theory and Media Studies. Martha assigned Herbert Marcuse's *One-Dimensional Man*, Walter Benjamin's "The Work of Art in the Age of Mechanical Reproduction," and "The Culture Industry: Enlightenment as Mass Deception," by Theodor Adorno and Max Horkheimer.

"The Culture Industry: Enlightenment as Mass Deception," a critical *tour de force*, combined high modernism and Marxism to level a withering one-two-punch on mass culture. The authors shared an elitism with high modernists like T.S Eliot, exhibiting a contempt for the cultural consumption of the masses. However, as Marxists, their sympathy supposedly lay with the masses themselves. The primary culprit is capitalism, not consumer taste. Exactly like other industries, culture is now mass-produced. Cultural goods are industrial products. Although they might present stylistic flourishes – in the stray shock of hair of the male film star, or in the syncopation of jazz – cultural products exhibit homogeneity and erase all signs of individuality – in the artistry, the artists, and in their consumers. Most importantly, the ultimate yield is not the cultural products themselves, but rather the formatting of leisure time and thereby the consciousness of the consumer-producer. Without this formatting, the authors hint, capitalism would falter because it would fail to reproduce the workforce. To ensure compliance, the culture industry eviscerates vestiges of individuality, transforming its targets into walking-talking replicas of the system itself.

The impact of this essay on me was both "enlightenment" and devastation. I felt as if I had been let in on a secret revealed only to a select few. At the same time, the essay rendered me akin to the mass-culture consumers it described. It eradicated any remaining conceit I held of possessing individuality. "Howl," Allen Ginsberg's poetic version of the same nightmare scenario, retained a sense of humor and betrayed signs of self-consciousness of its own peculiarity. It left open an escape hatch from its terrifying vision. But Adorno and Horkheimer's prose – with its "totalizing," surgical, clinical, analytical, and merciless tone and diction – acted like decryption code. It hacked into my head and planted a bug.

"I CAN'T GET NO (THEORETICAL) SATISFACTION"

The course continued through a vast canon of theory to follow, including postmodern theory. Analogous to the British pop invasion beginning in the 1960s, the invasion of the institutions of U.S. higher education (and its professoriate's and students' minds) by French cultural, gender, linguistic, literary, and social theory, later known collectively as postmodern, began in the late 1970s. Jacques Derrida, Jean-François Lyotard, Jean Baudrillard, and Michel Foucault were to the French theoretical invasion what the Beatles, the Rolling Stones, The Kinks, and the Yardbirds were to the British pop invasion. Consider these two invasions belated cultural gifts, tokens of appreciation bequeathed the U.S.

by the respective nations – for the crucial role that the U.S. played defending them from the Nazis.

Postmodern theory had first reached North America in the form of deconstruction, as expounded by the theoretical writing of French philosopher Jacques Derrida and literary scholar (and Nazi sympathizer) Paul de Man. Deconstruction was first taken up by members of the faculty in English at Yale. In addition to de Man, J. Hillis Miller, Harold Bloom, and Geoffrey Hartman were the early adopters. Despite differences, the four horsemen came to be known as the Yale Critics. The wave of French postmodern theory continued with the work of poststructuralists Jean-François Lyotard, Jean Baudrillard, Michel Foucault, the psychoanalytic theorist Jacques Lacan, and psychoanalytic feminists Luce Irigaray and Julia Kristeva (the last recently outed by the Bulgarian government as an agent during the communist era).

The structuralist linguist Ferdinand de Saussure had pointed out the arbitrary character of language in relation to its referents. For example, the word "tree" has no necessary relation to the particular kind of plant known as a "tree." Likewise, signifiers (words) are only meaningful in relation to and as different from other signifiers; their meaning derives not from anything intrinsic, or from any necessary connection to what they refer to, but only through their difference from other words. (In another form of structuralism, the American linguist Noam Chomsky had suggested that a deep structure of language undergirds and informs all languages. This underlying structure consists of functional universals and the units of various languages spill into them like so much liquid linguistic plastic into prefabricated molds.)

Saussure laid the groundwork for deconstruction and other forms of post-structuralism. According to poststructuralists, language is not a closed system with determinant structures and fixed relationships to referents but rather is characterized by "polysemy," or the endless proliferation of meaning. The semiotician Roland Barthes suggested that the only texts that are closed or rather that attempt to appear closed are ideologies – political, religious, and other "myths" (see *Mythologies*, 1957) that attempt to impose social, political, or theological closure on meaning. These include not only national and religious myths but also Marxism and the Enlightenment "myth" of reason and progress.

In *Of Grammatology* (1967), his inaugural book on deconstruction, Derrida wrote (in)famously that "there is no outside of text." By this, he meant that while language has generally been regarded as pointing to an ontological realm exterior to it, language actually has no natural or inevitable connection to anything beyond itself. Thus, the quest for knowledge and meaning using language ends with "mere" language itself.

The poststructuralist view of history, as expressed by its foremost historian, Michel Foucault, follows from its view of language as open-ended, arbitrary, and dependent on chance. Like language, history is marked not by continuity, repetitions, and universal patterns but rather "ruptures," breaks in continuity and order. Like language, historical events are arbitrary, aleatory, and peculiar.

Further, and perhaps most importantly, the poststructuralist breaking of the link between the signifier and its referent, between the word and the object it represents, suggests that language is autonomous and "literary." By this, poststructuralism suggests that language exhibits a stand-alone character; it is a system independent of the object world. As poststructuralists see it, the "literariness" of language ultimately threatens to undermine its epistemological reliability. According to poststructuralists, from the recognition that language has no natural referent it follows that attaining knowledge of the object world is foreclosed, or at least that knowledge cannot be represented in any definitive form. Of course, as I soon understood, it does not follow from the arbitrary character of language that knowledge is impossible. Once we assign meanings to words and link them tightly to referents, a relationship between words or other signifiers and their assigned objects is established and the linguistic or other symbolic system is more or less reliable. For example, the URLs of websites are arbitrary. But once specific locations are used to designate particular sites with particular and relatively predictable content, the URLs, and the World Wide Web at large, become systemically integral and relatively stable.

The postmodern theoretical understanding of language as open-ended and opposed to the closure of "totalizing" ideological systems explains postmodern politics. While postmodern theory does derive from the political left in France, it is definitely not Marxist. The difference is often lost on critics of postmodernism, such as my friend Jordan Peterson, who is too eager to call postmodern theory "neo-Marxism" and thus to equate it with its leftist predecessor. In fact, postmodern theory can be understood as the philosophical response to the failure of Marxism – in the student uprising of 1968. After the student movement failed to overturn the "totality" of the capitalist system, postmodern thinkers denied the very idea of a social totality and therefore the possibility of opposing it. Some came to see all attempts to impose a totality, whether such a totality were opposed to capitalism or not, as totalitarian. Against totalizing responses like Marxism, postmodern thinkers sought to undermine the structures of language, or to engage in other limited tactics of subversion. After the student movement ended in failure, the mass politics of the streets were abandoned and postmodern theorists like Roland Barthes, Michel de Certeau, and Michel Foucault sought alternatives in discursive subversion, in cunning tactics for surviving and subtly subverting capitalism, or in local institution-directed activism, respectively. While postmodern theory began as anti-capitalist, for postmodern theorists the enemy is any totalizing worldview or belief system, including political and social alternatives aimed at taking on the system as a whole – like Marxism.

Jean-François Lyotard, the philosopher who formally named the new theoretical impulse, was the most explicit in this regard. His book *The Postmodern Condition: A Report on Knowledge* (1979) formalized the postmodern critique and rejection of "master-narratives of legitimation." Master-narratives include narratives of liberation but also what Lyotard took to be a master-narrative – science – or any other major narrative that postulates a teleology or ultimate goal as either possible or desirable.

Despite the postmodern abandonment of Marxism, at this point, I considered myself a Marxist, albeit an "academic Marxist" – theoretically anti-capitalist based on Marxist analyses but uninvolved in direct political activity. I believed that the "totality" of social relations and interactions – including all cultural, economic, and political activity – could be best comprehended in terms of the totalizing, systemic structures of capitalism. The French Marxist theorist Louis Althusser cinched this comprehensiveness. In his "Ideology and Ideological State Apparatuses" (1970), which Martha assigned, Althusser translated structuralism into Marxist terms, and Marxism into structuralist terms. His "Ideology" essay neatly classifies the social totality in terms of the Marxist "base-superstructure" model. The productive capacities that directly meet material needs are referred to as the "base" or "infrastructure." The infrastructure includes the production of such goods as clothing, food, housing, transportation, and so on. On the other hand, the "superstructure" refers to the means of cultural production. The superstructure embraces most of education, entertainment, law, media, and religion, among other elements. Following Marx, Althusser argued that, under capitalism, the real role of the superstructure is to maintain the established order, especially ensuring that the relations of production (who does what) are expressed as class relations (who owns and controls what). For Marxists, class relations divide into two broad categories: the workers (proletariat) and the owners of the means of production (capitalists). According to Althusser, superstructural elements principally serve an ideological function – ultimately guaranteeing the systematic reproduction of a class structure, keeping the essential arrangement of productive relations and social relations the same, day after day. A tiny minority, the capitalist class, dominates the vast majority, the working class, through the ownership and control of productive capacities. This minority controls and consumes resources well out of proportion of their numbers.

According to Marxist theory, superstructural elements work by naturalizing, rationalizing, or, as I would learn later in the case of postmodern culture, ironizing the class system and the social order. To naturalize social reality is to make it appear inevitable and "just-so," like nature itself. Ideology works by transforming social relations into "natural" categories. For example, Marxists argue that "natural rights," such as the property rights, are not natural at all but rather cultural, economic, historical – political arrangements supported by a particular socioeconomic structure. Ironizing the social order has become a typical approach in postmodern culture or "late" capitalism. In a *New York Times* article, "How to Live Without Irony," Christy Wampole writes: "Advertising, politics, fashion, television: almost every category of contemporary reality exhibits this will to irony." By making fun of themselves, ads, politicians, and television shows preempt criticism and assure the complicity of consumers, voters, and audiences. For example, the sitcom *The Office* works by shamelessly exposing its characters' meaningless lives, thus preempting criticism of the show's frivolous plotlines, and likely reducing the anxiety of workers who share such banal existences.

My embrace of Marxism made no real practical difference at this point. I had never been involved in practical politics and I was not about to become involved any time soon. If anything, Marxism only increased the cynicism that I'd long held for a political system that seemed irrelevant to me and my life on the ground. I enjoyed Marxist theory – while ironically exploiting a "bourgeois" academic niche. Theory appealed to me intellectually. As an academic Marxist, I figured that my role was an ideological one. As a cultural producer, I might intervene in the superstructure to effect indirect change to ideology.

But, by this time, I had already become a postmodern subject. The "master narrative" of Marxism would not subsist within my consciousness unalloyed. Although Marxism displaced vestiges of other religious belief, vanquishing master narratives vying for allegiance, it was integrated within an overall postmodern framework. I was a postmodern subject because I acknowledged that although compelling, Marxist theory was necessarily incomplete. I retained postmodern theory as a "supplement," a word given new significance by Derrida; as a supplement, it served as both an addition to Marxism, and as a possible substitute for it – something that might come in handy, if or when needed. Postmodern theory's appeal to me was precisely that of *différance* – the word Derrida coined to signify both difference and deferral. *Différance* suggests the impossibility of interpretative finality (endless difference of meaning), as well as the deferral of satisfaction akin to the ever-unfulfilled consumer under consumer capitalism – "I can't get no (theoretical) satisfaction." The allure of postmodern theory's *différance* overwrote any impulse I may have had for theoretical closure. If becoming a "theory head," as it had earlier been called, required a thorough understanding of Marxism and Critical Theory, it also required a more than a passing familiarity with postmodern theory. The latter supplemented one's tool kit and might provide escape hatches from the "totality," like Ginsberg's poetry had done for me previously – a space for "the play of signifiers," a "ludic" valve for letting off the pressure of systemic steam.

ACQUIRING CULTURAL CAPITAL

Martha stuck a Post-it note on the last page of my survey and analyses of the corpus of theory, which read: "Mike – A thorough and often insightful set of analyses. They reflect an impressive grasp of the whole domain of 'critical theory!'" Ironically, in light of my earlier predispositions and "unconscious" allegiances, even before the end of the Cultural Criticism course, I found myself enrolled in the small corps of "Cultural Studies mavens" within the department. I was now part of an intellectual *avant-garde*, one of "those people" that "other people" in the department did not understand. These "other people" were either too stupid to understand us, were too indelicate or flat-footed to recognize our brilliance – or, what was much worse, they were cultural conservatives, even reactionaries.

I remember a good-natured argument with Joel, one of the more traditional literary types among the English Ph.D. students. Joel was a hale, athletic guy in his early thirties who assiduously cultivated a healthy social life and a realist's perspective regarding the excesses, idiosyncrasies, and conceits of the field. For example, he made no apologies for his "heteronormativity," to say the least. He neither claimed to be an "ally," or a male feminist.

Joel challenged my leftist enthusiasm. At one point, he asked me: "But don't you believe in the will to power?" I'd read a lot of Nietzsche, especially in the previous summer. I'd acknowledged the *modus operandi* of the will to power and agreed with Nietzsche's position that socialism represents a resentment ideology and a stealthy will to power. But now I dismissed Nietzsche as the last of the Romantic individualists. I also had a spirited discussion with Paula Makris. She challenged my understanding of morality as historically contingent and determined by ruling-class interests. Paula seemed to suggest that morals might be universal, a notion that was utterly *passé*. The notion of universals had been made *passé* by cultural relativism but also by the understanding that class interests determined moral codes. The dominant morality was the morality of the dominant class.

The friction involved not only other grad students but also professors. When I took classes taught by Martha's colleagues, I faced a degree of antipathy and suspicion due to my reputation as one of her acolytes. At the start of each semester, I would transfer from course to course until I found professors who weren't overtly hostile to me. I finally found professors Gary Stonum and Bill Siebenschuh quite hospitable and receptive. Stonum particularly appreciated my theoretical and cultural knowledge, and Siebenschuh encouraged my theory-laden interpretation of George Eliot's novel, *Middlemarch*.

The Cultural Studies and Theory coterie included my closest friend at Case, John Kuijper, a young, gay and optimistic student from Seattle whose leanings were leftist but who held the fashionable postmodernist position that Marxism was a totalitarian master-narrative. John left after finishing his M.A. and became a high school teacher. It included Mary Ann Cole, a devotee of Jacques Lacan, the French psychoanalytical theorist who, to use shorthand, translated Freud's sexual-biological determinism into a symbolic system. Being a Lacanian required incredible dedication, since Lacanian theoretical writing is copious, ambiguous, and dense, and moreover, probably useless. No one who knows it at all ever claims to know it all and the perspective has no real place in contemporary psychotherapy. I have never since heard of or from Mary Ann Cole. Marc Abraham was another leftist-but-not-quite-Marxist among the crew. He relished postmodern theory. He and I gave a presentation on Michel de Certeau's *The Practice of Everyday Life* (1984), a peculiar amalgam of qualitative sociology and cultural anthropology, and also a sort of sinister (literally "leftist") handbook for postmodern political practice, or the tactics that the weak could employ against the strong in ongoing subversive campaigns that never remotely approach revolution. Marc later dropped out of the Ph.D. program to pursue something more practical; I never knew just what. Paula Makris was another fellow traveler. Although not a Martha follower as such, her interests lay in post-colonialism, which turned out to be prescient on her part, since postcolonial theory became the rage at about the time that she (and I) went on the job market. Dr. Paula Makris is now an Associate Professor of English and Department Chair at Wheeling Jesuit University. Senior members of Martha's camp included Lisa Maruca. Lisa followed closely in Martha's footsteps by historicizing authorship, discussed below, taking such study back into the late seventeenth century. Dr. Lisa Maruca is now an Associate Professor at Wayne State University.

Gaining admittance to this camp demanded ardor and loyalty but also returned compensation, the kind of compensation that Pierre Bourdieu, the French postmodernist sociologist, called "cultural capital." Cultural capital is the kind of capital that – unlike the material capital held by the (vulgar) owners of the means of production (capitalists) – includes the possession of "property" of symbolic value. Elements of symbolic cultural capital include esoteric knowledge (such as knowledge of postmodern theory), credentials inaccessible to the vast majority (such as a Ph.D. in Literary and Cultural Theory), subtle mannerisms and modes of expression (including the proper tics, or, emulating the Slovenian superstar of theory, Slavoj Žižek, greasy hair and the repetition of such characteristic expressions as "and so on and so forth"), having counterintuitively "wrong" connections (such as a friendship with the owner of a particularly deplorable business), the reading of particularly obscure texts (although most obscurity doesn't count), and so on and so forth. Cultural capital can be spent in several ways. One can spend it subtly, with a nearly imperceptible snobbery, such as that reserved and mildly sneering disdain for members of a rearguard camp. Of course, cultural capital was exchanged for professional and interpersonal advantage.

Figure 5: Slovenian superstar of theory, Slavoj Žižek, apparently pointing to his greasy hair as a form of cultural capital. (Photo/UnB Agência)

THE (DE)CONSTRUCTION OF AUTHORSHIP

Expected to remain onboard the theory boat, in the spring semester of 1994, I took Martha's seminar, "The Construction of Authorship." Right from the jump, it became clear that this course involved debunking the cultural status of "the author" – and elevating that of "the theorist." Authors had been generally regarded as the sources of original works. But, as Roland Barthes pointed out in "The Death of the Author" (1968), originality was a myth: "We know now that a text is not a line of words releasing a single 'theological' meaning (the 'message' of the Author-God) but a multi-dimensional space in which a variety of writings, none of them original, blend and clash." All writing was thus merely montage, collage, and/or reportage.

Deconstructing the author was akin to religious iconoclasm. In "What Is an Author?" (1969), Foucault noted that for several centuries, authors had been celebrated as individuals of extraordinary talent, as the founts of creative bounty. But authors actually serve as lids on the containers of culture. They are the corks in the jug, veritable cultural prohibitionists. The author functions, or, turning the person of the author into a textual artifact, "the author function," actually serves to control and restrict discourse, determining just who is authorized to produce "fiction," broadly construed. While we think of authors as sources of new, original, and unlimited meaning, the real role of authors is to stymie the proliferation of meaning. The function of the author is thus an ideological one because the author's reputed function is "the opposite of his historically real function." The author is not the source of meaning but rather a limiter of it. As their supposed sources, authors laid claim to the ownership of works. But, in fact, authors do not create works. Works create their authors! The author is a function of the text, a product of language, not its source. What's more, the individual subject itself, of which the author is but a type – that is, individual personhood – is a textual production! Subjectivity itself is a function of language. This is the quintessential post-structuralist conception of "the subject," or the human person, the self. The self is a product of text. This notion forms the basis of the transgender theoretical position that one's gender identity depends, finally, on naming.

I noted to myself that both Barthes and Foucault had put their names on these essays, despite their objections to dominance of "the author" and his ownership of texts.

In the introduction to his essay, "What Is an Author?," Foucault writes: "I shall not offer here a sociohistorical analysis of the author's persona. Certainly it would be worth examining how the author became individualized in a culture like ours ..." Foucault did not want to undertake such heavy lifting himself. But in the gap that he identified and left open, Martha Woodmansee descried her academic niche. (Her discovery is characteristic of how many academic niches, at least in English Studies, are found and exploited.) In what became a seminal and very well-cited essay, "The Genius and the Copyright: Economic and Legal Conditions of the Emergence of the 'Author'" (1984), Martha began to tap this vein and occupy this niche. She examined the economic, legal, and theoretical contexts for the emergence of the modern author as such. Her major book, *The Author, Art, and The Market: Rereading the History of Aesthetics* (1994), treated transformations in aesthetic theories of eighteenth-century German and British philosophers and aesthetes as functions of economic, legal, and social forces. In this way, she tackled Immanuel Kant, wrestling the philosopher to the ground of history, and ultimately, theory. She managed to explain philosophical and aesthetic theory in terms of the economic and legal factors. For example, the late nineteenth-century notion of "art for art's sake" was simply a function of the market, a resentful and otiose reaction to the emergence of mass culture.

Once exposed to the theoretical and historical underpinnings of modern authorship, I begrudgingly began to surrender any belief in myself as an "author." Although I felt disburdened of a great weight, the onus of the "author construct" as it was called, I also experienced a significant loss, akin to the loss of a long-time lover. I ran through several cycles of the stages of grief – denial, rage, bargaining, and depression. At last, I reached acceptance, of a kind. But then I asked myself: "Should I accept something that's not necessarily true?" There I was again, back at denial. Eventually, however, I managed to convince myself that the conceit of authorship was untenable. The intellectual ballast contained in The Construction of Authorship course had blown massive holes in the literary enterprise for me. The author and authorship themselves were based on cultural, legal, and ideological fictions. How could anyone knowingly perform an "ideological function?" I wondered. And yet I continued to grieve the death of a ghost.

LIKE A VIRUS

My courses at Case Western also included seminars in Milton, the American Renaissance (with Gary Stonum), Composition Theory (with Judy Oster), Renaissance Theater (with Tom Bishop), and an independent study in the Victorian novel (with Bill Siebenschuh), plus one more course of Martha's entitled, "The New Economic Criticism."

The New Economic Criticism may be understood as representing another phalanx of postmodern theoretical ambition infiltrating yet another discipline, this time, economics. On its face, the endeavor referred to a new interdisciplinary collaboration between economists and literary theorists to revise thinking within both fields. For the literary theorists, economics might be shown to consist of "narratives," rather than standing as an autonomous scientific field. Economics would thus yield to the critiques of literary theory. Some adventuresome (or perhaps resentful) economists seemed to find the prospect alluring and welcomed the new postmodern colonialists with open arms. The opportunity to treat economics as literature promised these economists a kind of cultural capital not normally available to those whose chief concern involved the pedestrian matters of the market. Now their own work might be regarded as literature. The postmodern colonialists did come bearing gifts: they introduced economic models likely unfamiliar to economists, including the ancient "gift economy," discovered by the French cultural anthropologist Marcel Mauss, and the symbolic economics of French sociologist Pierre Bourdieu.

The course work was connected to a conference hosted by the English department and run by the Society for Critical Exchange, which Martha directed. We read a massive load of background material, and then all of the conference papers. John Kuijper helped Martha to run the conference, and I filled in and delivered a paper on Wallace Stevens, written by a presenter who couldn't make it. After it ended, Martha asked me to write a review of the conference as a whole. On the last page of the paper, Martha wrote what had been to date the highest praise she'd heaped upon my work: "This is a tremendous exploration of relations between these two disciplines. You've an excellent grasp of the whole terrain, including its history, and identify the salient features of a new (vs. old) economic criticism ... Fine work!"

Despite such praise, I felt uneasy about the objectives of the New Economic Criticism. Would it serve as yet another means of liquidating culture, a form of arbitrage like that practiced by George Soros across national borders, a melting of the specific qualities of culture into a base economic metal? Would it thus become yet another means for debunking the status of literary and other cultural objects? At the same time, I worried that the New Economic Criticism represented yet another means by which postmodern theory would infiltrate discipline after discipline, and, like a virus, replicate itself using the DNA of its hosts. I, for one, had long been infected.

Incidentally, as they sat in a U.S. airport waiting to deplane, Derrida and de Man reportedly remarked that deconstruction was a virus they were about to unleash on their unwary American hosts.

Rather than staying at Case Western for the Ph.D., I decided to find a program more highly ranked and also more theoretically diverse and extensive. Martha had been effectively running, solo, a Cultural Studies and Critical Theory program within an otherwise traditional English department. While some professors and grad students had "Stop/ Deconstruction!" signs on their doors, Martha was one of the bulldozers, although not at all technically a deconstructionist. It was clear that many in the faculty did not appreciate her incommensurate influence. As I've suggested, the issues faculty had with Martha sometimes extended to her acolytes, like me. And, I didn't want to fight the whole the English faculty for the remainder of my graduate school career.

I was accepted by several schools and chose Carnegie Mellon University's (CMU) program in Literary and Cultural Theory/Studies (LCT/S). Given the understanding of the field I'd gained already, plus the recognition and high praise from Martha and others, I felt confident about diving deeper into the field, into even more arcane, stranger postmodernist waters – taking another, much riskier plunge. I put everything on the line to pursue a Ph.D. in LCT/S at CMU.

CHAPTER 6
EVEN MORE ARCANE, STRANGER
POSTMODERN WATERS

VILLAINS AND LAUGHING STOCKS

A S A PH.D. STUDENT at CMU, I didn't deal much with many of the students, or much of the drama surrounding them. Likewise, recollections of my Ph.D. studies are necessarily much more textual than anecdotal. The lack of narrative elements will yield the advantage of treating the texts more closely but necessarily entails the disadvantage of seeming somewhat disembodied. Yet this disembodied, textually focused discussion is perhaps more apropos of postmodern theoretical existence than anything else.

The introductory part of my graduate studies, the Masters in English Literature, had involved coverage of literary periods and a theoretical smorgasbord. But once enrolled in the Ph.D. program in LCT/S at CMU, I focused on various theoretical paradigms in classes devoted to each: Marxisms, The Frankfurt School of Critical Theory, Feminisms, Semiotics, Poststructuralism (including Queer Theory), Theories of the Subject, Deconstruction, Postcolonial Theory, Science Studies, and the Rhetoric of Science.

Although theory primers often compared theoretical perspectives to different "lenses" through which one might read a text or other cultural object, one was not really supposed to try them on like pairs of eyeglasses at the optical department. In fact, one was not quite able to. First, each critical method represented a voluminous corpus and required a serious commitment to its perspective. Regardless of the school or camp, the theoretical writing almost inevitably confronted the reader with a welter of verbal, conceptual, historical, and referential density. Second, these theoretical camps vied against each other for "hegemony," while competition raged within them. Everyone aimed to represent a distinctive break from predecessors, while remaining within a recognizable fold. Finally, some theoretical paradigms had identity entrance requirements. For example, as a feminist friend Mary Ann Cole had kindly explained to me, a "man" should not "do feminism," until or unless every "woman" in the field has found publication space and a professorial station. His work cannot displace the work of a woman in publication and he cannot take a job teaching feminism as long as a single woman needs a position. The admonition reminds me of those foreboding parking signs in New York: "Don't even think of parking here!"

Obviously, I had by now known and accepted the premise that English Studies was a battlefield of "textual politics," and that the players made no bones about their agendas. Previously, critics in the field, like the old New Critics with their plodding close reading of texts, had pretended to be neutral, but their neutrality was merely a thin scrim for cultural domination. Dead white men had ruled the English canon long enough. But this was only the most flagrant of offenses. Other suspects were singled out for prosecution – including an exclusive focus on the text itself (New Criticism), assuming the centrality or superiority of European culture (Eurocentrism), implicitly endorsing heterosexuality as a norm (heteronormativity), believing that humanity is exceptional and that individual humans have unitary selves (humanism), believing in an essence of human nature and/or in the essence of essential types of humans such as racial groups and women and men (essentialism), the belief that neutral knowledge is discoverable by scientific means (positivism), the belief that words might faithfully represent an external reality (logocentrism), and the privileging of the masculine in the construction of meaning (phallogocentrism) – among others. Every one of these notions or beliefs has been treated as a villain, a laughing stock, or both.

Let's take positivism, an easy target for postmodern theorists. I've never seen the word "positivism" (or "positivist") used positively in a postmodern text. But the banishment of positivism did not begin with postmodernism. It started in the nineteenth century. The sobriquet has stood for a plodding empiricism and an exclusive devotion to facts, like the approach lampooned by Dickens with the character Gradgrind in *Hard Times* (1848): "'In this life, we want nothing but Facts, sir; nothing but Facts!'" It also signifies the domination of "instrumental rationality" over life, as it was characterized within Critical Theory by the Frankfurt School. Even the cultural conservative Allan Bloom disparaged it: "The academic character of the philosophy departments, with their tired and tiresome methodology and positivism, had caused people interested in the perennial and live questions about man [sic] to migrate to the social sciences." Positivism has served as a textual placeholder for postmodernists, a whipping boy to thrash as they closed in on the real culprits.

THE GENDER JACKPOT

Now for a truly dangerous villain. "Phallogocentrism" is a peculiarly postmodern bogey. It took center stage in the Feminisms seminar at CMU, taught by Professor Kristina Straub. Phallogocentrism refers to the phallus, a word that the post-Freudian French psychoanalytic theorist Jacques Lacan used not to refer to the penis but to the symbolic authority of masculinity. The phallus is thus the (largely invisible) magic wand of masculine authority and power. Phallogocentrism includes the root, "logo," the word for "the Word" itself, and has Biblical overtones. Since Aristotle, logos has been associated with language but also with reason. The two roots – masculinity and linguistic rationality – combine with "centric" to signify the domination of masculine linguistic rationality – over nature, coded as feminine, and over the feminine itself. While "toxic masculinity," the bastardized social justice version of man-disease, renders the accused a boor, given the rational and linguistic prowess it ascribes to the thought criminal, phallogocentrism might be received as compliment.

My first encounter with Kristina Straub seemed to have been conditioned by phallogocentrism, or at least a perception of it. I sensed some wariness if not a slight hostility during our first in-person encounter. It was during orientation to the program. Kristina and I walked beside each other, along with a group of new and older grad students, bouncing nerd-like down the hallway. As we descended the dark, sloping corridor of Baker Hall from the English department to a nearby classroom, Kristina maintained a disconcerting silence, even after I tried small talk to loosen things up. I had observed her chatting in friendly tones with other students. I might have taken the guarded demeanor for reserve with strangers if she hadn't been jovial with the two other new Ph.D. students, Dana Gliserman and Michael Haber.

I believe her coolness toward me had to do with a book review I'd written and published in the *Pittsburgh Post-Gazette* in late August 1997, just before the start of the semester. As Danny, the business manager for the English department told me, the piece couldn't be missed. It covered a whole page, top and bottom, and included a huge, quarter-page photograph. It was my review of the massive biography, *Virginia Woolf* (1996), by University of Oxford Professor Hermione Lee. After heaping praise on the biography, I referred to what I thought was its inordinate length (893 pages). I then tried to account for this prodigious volume. (I was also secretly airing a grievance, since I only made $200 per review, regardless of how long the book.) I remarked that "'life-writing' on such a scale turns into a fetish. The question that comes to mind is: What motivates such a massive hagiography?" In other words, why do we pay so much attention to authors and artists, and why so excessively in this particular case? I went on to offer a Freudian interpretation: "Freud claimed that Western civilization's concerns with art have more to do with artists than with art itself. The high valorization of artists and authors involves, he maintained, an idealization and subsequent dethroning of father figures. The artist or author is thus both a representation of the father as well as an Oedipal hero who kills the father, a theory that fits with the centuries-long male-centeredness of the arts and letters ... Lee's biography thus appears to be making up for the libraries of commentary devoted to male artists and authors."

I knew very well that nearly all feminists repudiated Freud's "biologism," as it was derogatorily called in literary studies and gender studies – his understanding of personality, and social and sex relations, in terms of a sexuality predicated on anatomy. Further, I knew that Freud's theory of the Oedipal Complex – in which the male child fantasizes about murdering his father for love of his mother but fears castration by the father and so (ideally for Freud) redirects his libidinal impulses to their "proper objects" – was seen as setting the terms not only for individual psychology but for the entire social order, for civilization itself. In the case of the masculine, the crisis ends in homosocial bonding with the father, and male bonding between men in a "fraternity of equals." But Freud couldn't figure out what to do with women. He left the female out of the fraternity of equals, an exclusion based on "lack." In the case of the female child, her redirection from the pre-Oedipal love of the mother to the love of the father involves a violent disruption of attachment, as she is wrested away from the mother, while the love of the father is effectively "forced" on her. The suggestions of interrupted homoeroticism and staged paternal rape had not been lost on feminists.

Freud's phallogocentrism had been derided by feminists for decades. I knew this, and ultimately referred to Virginia Woolf as "an Oedipal female," a notion Freud introduced in his later work, when he no longer reduced psychodynamics to anatomy. As an Oedipal female, Virginia Woolf rejected her father, and rather than reproducing children, devoted her energies to producing literature, writing that symbolically killed him. This reading was consistent with Woolf's rejection of the writing of her father, Leslie Stephen, and his attempts to render faithful, "positivist" biographies of famous Victorians in "life writing." Woolf argued that biography always involves fiction, and fiction, autobiography. Several feminists and gender/sex theorists, including Gayle Rubin, whom we read in Kristina Straub's Feminist Theory, reclaimed the female Oedipus and reinterpreted the Freudian version of the Oedipal drama. Yet this feminist revisionism did not come across in my review. Instead, I was likely read as a Freudian, a biological determinist.

During the first or second meeting of the Feminist Theory class, I asked a question about the reading. Kristina responded by referring to my apparent "essentialism" and "biological determinism," and seemed to mockingly suggest that I must believe in retrograde gender ideas like the reality of sex difference. The idea was preposterous! I balked. This was far from my view! I spent the remainder of the semester disabusing Kristina of such a dreadful notion. I was not a regressive biological determinist. No, I embraced and promoted social and linguistic gender constructivism (or constructionism), with fervor!

By way of introducing gender constructionism or constructivism, it is useful to recall that before the second half of the 20th century, the term "gender" predominantly referred to the coding of words as feminine or masculine. In 1955, the sexologist John Money seeded the gender jackpot when he introduced the term "gender roles." Soon, gender began to describe the set of behaviors and personality traits conventionally connected with sex (difference) in humans. Some feminists used the term from the 1970s onward to refer to the social roles, behavioral expectations, and treatment typically expected from and doled out to males and females. These gender feminists described sex as a skeletal "coat rack" on which the accouterments of gender hung like so many tailored coats, scarves, and hats. Meanwhile, gender was a "social construct" – the woven product of socialization and social environment, as opposed to nature. As a social product, gender might be refashioned along different lines by reconfiguring socialization processes and altering social relations.

Yet when gender-critical feminists first defined gender as a social construct, they didn't mean to suggest that gender could be altered arbitrarily on the basis of individual will. They saw gender constructs as obdurate social categories that had been established by long-standing conventions and enforced in multiple, almost inscrutable ways. Gender was no less real for being socially constructed. Undermining gender involved a long, arduous social struggle. And gender-critical feminists figured sex and gender as tightly coupled. As I discuss in Chapter 10, the transgender movement has since turned gender into a matter of individual whimsy, treating gender "choice" like an ice-cream flavor preference. Meanwhile, no one in the trans movement ever suggests that they decided to change their gender to "appreciate" the lowlights of a gender. And although transgender theory figures gender as non-binary, it nevertheless casts genders in stereotypical bodies and vestures, which then need to be swapped.

I found the idea of the social construction of gender gratifying and I must admit that I enjoyed gender constructionism, partly for its shock value. In the '90s, few people outside of the walls of the academy had heard of such a notion. Gretchen and my non-academic friends clung to what I then saw as hopelessly archaic, reductionist explanations of gender – or even sex difference. Their ideas derived from evolutionary psychology, unconscious forms of biological determinism, or simply, sexist stereotypes. Or so I thought at the time. I had arguments with my friend, Jeff Schwartz, who had imbibed evolutionary psychology and held that gender was "hardwired" biologically through the evolutionary selection of traits associated with "the two sexes." The horror! The horror! In English Studies, Women's Studies, and Gender Studies departments, the mere hint of such determinism would be sniffed out, with the possible consequence of career death for whoever might lend it voice. But my adoption of gender constructionism was not simply pragmatic or tactical. I had been firmly convinced of the social and linguistic construction of gender. I wasn't merely play-acting.

I proved capable of entertaining the various schools of feminist and gender theoretical thought, including second-wave Marxist-feminism, radical feminism, third-wave feminism, queer theory, and gender and transgender theory. But the landscape of radical feminist, queer, gender, and transgender theory was a minefield. Like Barack Obama during a press conference, I sorted slowly through my language options and selected words with the utmost deliberation and care. Deference was always the fallback position, especially for the straight white male. Although the term "mansplaining" was twenty years off, great peril attended the straight white male who stepped on the toes of the Other. Trespassing an Other's gender identity or sexuality turf, failing to defer to the experience of Others, could land one in rhetorical, social, and ultimately professional hot water. While one never knew what might irk, one could be sure that recalcitrance and repeated transgressions of acceptable feminist and gender orthodoxy would lead to permanent banishment.

Meanwhile, as the readings for the course made evident, the internecine battles within feminist, queer, and transgender theory were routinely ferocious and caustic. For example, in a chapter from her book *Deviant Eyes, Deviant Bodies*, Chris Straayer ridiculed psychoanalytic feminism, particularly feminist adoptions of Lacanian psychoanalysis. Despite Lacan's promise that as a symbolic relation rather than a biological one, the subordination of women through phallogocentrism might be undone, Straayer argued that "psychoanalysis is useful for describing the status quo: at the same time, such description could function as a reinforcement, as a lock against change." A comic illustration in Straayer's text has stayed with me for over twenty years. She described a scene from *Delirium* (1993), a short film by Mindy Faber informed by feminist theory. In one scene, Faber mocked psychoanalytic feminist theory by disguising herself as a man; wearing a plastic-nose-glasses-and-mustache disguise, she proceeded to breastfeed her male baby. As such, she mockingly suggested that the little man, believing Faber to be his father, or unsure, would see the father and mother as interchangeable and thus elude the Oedipal Complex and overthrow the patriarchy.

Soon, Kristina and I came to understand each other. She appreciated my writing and my oral contributions to class discussions. I understood the parameters of acceptable dialogue and the levels of sensitivity associated with the various points of orthodoxy. I worked hard to trace the nuances and differences, and also the confluences, of the wide and quite contentious field of feminist, queer, gender-critical, and transgender discourse. At the end of her comments on my paper about Gayle Rubin's "The Traffic in Women," Kristina made a remark that pleasantly surprises me to this day: "The place you end up in – questioning identity politics – is an interesting & productive way into some of the most difficult dilemmas posed in both feminist & l/g [lesbian/gay] theory. We're working w/a political system that privileges 'identity' – & yet our most powerful theoretical frameworks for challenging oppression call the concept into question." I agreed, and later developed a particular critique of identity politics that was published in a leftist webzine. I argued that fetishizing identity inevitably leads identity politics devotees into cul-de-sacs. Identity politics serves to reinforce and "reify" (or make into things) identity categories – to solidify the very categorizations that are considered sources of oppression. I argued that by making equality with other "privileged" groups the sole object of political activity – rather than overcoming of the constraining categories of identity – identity politics contributes to the strength of identity categories, and thus, lends force to their subordination. In other words, where the members of subordinated identity groups are concerned, most leftists do much more harm than good.

MUH KNOWLEDGE

That fall semester also included a seminar in the Frankfurt School of Critical Theory, taught by Dr. Sharon Ghamari-Tabrizi, a Post-Doctoral Fellow at CMU's Humanities Center. Dana Gliserman and Michael Haber also enrolled. Sharon had completed her Ph.D. in the History of Consciousness Program at U.C. Santa Cruz in 1993, and had been a student of Donna Haraway, the famous postmodernist Science Studies theorist. Sharon was clearly a brilliant thinker and an accomplished scholar, but her training in the History of Consciousness Program, considered flakey outside of Santa Cruz, had made her job search problematic. On her personal website, sharonghamari.com, Sharon euphemistically describes having been an "itinerant scholar" during her years in academia, when for eleven years she bounced around from one temporary position to another and from one university to another. When I met Donna Haraway at an annual Science and Literature Studies conference, I mentioned Sharon and my gratitude for having been a student of one of Haraway's brightest protégés. I then broached the topic of Sharon's academic misadventures. Haraway expressed bitterness that Sharon had fared so badly.

Sharon introduced the Frankfurt School by beginning with Immanuel Kant, Georg Wilhelm Friedrich Hegel, and the early Hungarian Soviet literary critic and Marxist philosopher, György Lukács. In his book, *History and Class Consciousness* (1923), Lukács introduced a form of epistemology that has had an outsized impact ever since, serving as a source for postmodern theory and social justice. The social justice notion that each person has their own truth based on their particular type of subordination can be traced to Lukács. He argued that the unique position of the working class within the social order and the relations of production provide the proletariat with a privileged vantage-point for discerning objective truth and called the theory "proletarian standpoint epistemology." Lukács argued that reality under capitalism is a single objective reality. But the proletarian has a peculiar relationship to objective reality. The objective world strikes the proletarian differently than it does the capitalist. Like the capitalist, the proletarian is a self-conscious subject. However, unlike the capitalist, the proletarian is also a commodity, an object for sale on the market. The proletarian's consciousness of the commodification of his selfhood contradicts his experience as living subject, a person with a subjective existence. The proletariat's "self-consciousness of the commodity" (that is himself) explains the working class's antagonism toward capitalism as Lukács saw it. While the proletariat fully grasps the contradiction of its self-conscious commodification, the class can only come to terms with the contradiction by upending and abolishing existing conditions.

In *The Science Question in Feminism* (1986), Sandra Harding adopted Lukács's proletarian standpoint epistemology and adapted it to feminism. Relegated to the caretaking of men, children, and themselves, women experience a deepened and unified sense of "hand, heart, and head" activity, and thus appreciate a deepened "sensuous, concrete, relational" access to the world. Their particular standpoint accords them an enhanced cognitive and perceptual grasp of objectivity.

Postmodernists later appropriated standpoint epistemology as it was siphoned through various identity filters. It is the root of the contemporary social justice belief in the connection between identity and knowledge. Social justice holds that membership in a subordinated identity group grants members exclusive access to particular knowledge, their own knowledge. Members of dominant identity groups cannot access or understand the knowledge of subordinated others. For example, a white "cishetero" male (a white straight man who accepts the gender that he was "assigned at birth") cannot have a black lesbian's experience and therefore can't access or understand her knowledge. Individuals within subordinated identity groups also have their own individual knowledge. For social justice believers, knowledge is personal, individual, and impenetrable to others. It is "muh knowledge." I call this notion of knowledge "epistemological solipsism." Under the social justice worldview, everyone is locked in an impenetrable identity chrysalis with access to a personal knowledge that no one else can reach.

In a recent *New York Times* op-ed entitled, "How Ta-Nehisi Coates Gives Whiteness Power," Thomas Chatterton Williams discusses what I am calling epistemological solipsism, which he calls "knowing-through-being" and "identity epistemology." Williams laments identity epistemology or knowing-through-being because it limits knowledge to members of particular identity categories and it slides seamlessly into "identity ethics" or "morality-through-being." Morality-through-being is believed to follow from knowing-through-being as the subordinated assumes the moral high ground on the basis of a superior knowledge standpoint deriving from subordinated status. Morality-through-being or identity-ethics results in a moral ranking in which the lowest on the totem pole is deemed a moral superior by virtue of her (previous) subordination. Through the kind of hierarchical inversion that Friedrich Nietzsche saw in Judaism, Christianity, and socialism, low status becomes high status.

Therefore, social justice ideology does not foster egalitarianism. Rank is maintained, only the bottom becomes the top when the totem pole of identity is inevitably flipped upside-down and stood on its head. (Rank is established on the basis of intersectionality, a grid for determining the number of ways that a subject is subordinated based on race, gender, sexual orientation, and so forth.) Is it any wonder then that social justice warriors compete valiantly for the status of "most subordinated" in the games derogatorily referred to as "the Oppression Olympics?" The race to the bottom is really a race to the top – although the race runs downhill.

How did Lukács's proletariat standpoint epistemology become an epistemological solipsism resulting in the inverted moral hierarchy of the contemporary social justice movement? While Lukács argued that the proletariat's material standpoint yielded the class unique access to objective truth, by the time it reached contemporary social justice, standpoint epistemology had already been stripped of any pretense to objective truth by postmodern theory. According to postmodern theory, the very idea of "objective truth" is a master narrative. Under social justice ideology, objective truth is a legacy of patriarchal white supremacy.

"TRANSGRESSING THE BOUNDARIES"

In the spring semester of 1998, I took another class with Sharon Ghamari-Tabrizi, "An Introduction to the Social Studies of Science," which proved pivotal for me. A few students from the Frankfurt School seminar also followed suit. This course also drew students from the

Ph.D. program in Rhetoric, including Peter Cramer and Craig Stewart. Because the study of rhetoric is deemed more practical than theory, the rhetoric Ph.D. students stood a much better chance in the job market upon finishing the degree. Like Peter and Craig, they were almost invariably less edgy and more conventional in outlook and appearance than those in my program. I appreciated them for the relief that they represented against the posturing and pretense of the LCT/S students' radicalism.

But the class attendees also included Samantha (Sam) and Meg, two intolerant and intolerable Ph.D. students a year or two ahead of me in LCT/S. After a couple weeks, this inseparable pair eventually took to heckling me, week after week, in the middle of class. From the back of the room, they made snorting and other noises when I began to speak. I think they may have taken exception to my language use, which apparently struck them as excessively recondite, and thus, I suppose, "phallogocentric." But at the time I had no idea what was going on. I couldn't think of anything I had done wrong, although I now know that I was guilty of the social justice version of original sin – the inexpiable sin of being born into white straight masculinity. This was the first time in my academic career that my identity posed a problem. It would not be the last.

In any case, "The Social Studies of Science" is otherwise called "Science, Technology and Society" (STS) or simply "Science Studies." Science Studies is an interdisciplinary field that draws mostly from the humanities and social sciences and includes postmodern theorists who have attempted to debunk the special epistemological and institutional status of science in order to assimilate it to other ordinary human activities. Sharon's syllabus described the course as a "review [of] the main theoretical approaches to the critique of scientific authority." It aimed at challenging the distinction between "scientific knowledge and the rest of human affairs."

We read Sandra Harding's *The Science Question in Feminism* as well as the bizarre new work by Sharon's mentor, Donna Haraway, entitled, *Modest_Witness@Second_Millennium.FemaleMan_Meets_OncoMouse: Feminism and Technoscience* (1997), and half a dozen other books. I've already discussed the prior and the latter can't be rendered conceptually without an overwrought commentary, as it intentionally merges with science fiction and it is bizarre. It's more important to lay down some of the fundamentals of the field.

The French postmodern anthropologist and sociologist Bruno Latour has been a major player in the field of Science Studies for almost forty years. In a co-written book, *Laboratory Life: The Social Construction of Scientific Facts* (1979), his first major contribution to the field, Latour teamed with Steve Woolgar for an in-situ study of laboratory science. *Laboratory Life* is an anthropological examination of a scientific laboratory as a strange but not altogether exotic culture. The assumed strangeness effect allowed Latour and Woolgar to see science's final product in terms of what they called "literary inscription" or writing. Despite Latour's subsequent break with the implications of "the social construction of scientific facts" arrived at in *Laboratory Life*, the first book is constructivist through and through. The anthropologists aimed to show that "the construction of scientific facts, in particular, is a process of generating texts whose fate (status, value, utility, facticity) depends on their subsequent interpretation." Latour and Woolgar thus reduced the objects of science to "text," just as Derrida had done with ontologies (ideas and concrete entities) in philosophy. (See Chapter 5.) Of course, a fallacy was at work. Latour and Woolgar's sleight of hand demonstrated that scientific facts exist only within texts – "there is no outside of text." But as with all magic tricks, the deception had taken place earlier, before we were looking. Latour and Woolgar stealthily conflated the knowledge of scientific facts – established in the process of science and expressed in language – and the reality referred to by that knowledge. Confusing knowledge and the objects of knowledge, our postmodern magicians seemed to make the material world itself disappear into the text. The error (or more likely the intentional prestidigitation) is known as the fallacy of reification – or treating an abstraction (like the knowledge of a fact) as equivalent to a concrete object or thing (like the object to which the knowledge refers).

Books like this eventually attracted the attention of battle-ready scientists, some of whom brought charges of radical relativism and epistemological nihilism (or the belief that knowledge is unattainable) against Science Studies. With *Higher Superstition: The Academic Left and its Quarrels with Science* (1994), biologist Paul R. Gross and mathematician Norman Levitt lobbed the first bomb of the scientific counter-insurgency. Admittedly somewhat simplified, Gross and Levitt's account nevertheless aptly rendered comprehensible the wide-ranging corpus of Science Studies. According to Gross and Levitt, Science Studies represented a stealth operation undertaken by academic leftist mischief-makers who attempted to dislodge science from its parapet in an institutional turf battle and a power play to undermine public trust in science. The authors saved their most trenchant attacks for the post-modern Science Studies contingent. The postmodern incursion into science, they claimed, represented "an attempt to bring science within its [postmodernism's] empire." Note, as these defenders of science saw it, the anti-science academic left posed a greater threat to science than any rightwing climate or evolutionary science deniers.

Higher Superstition was followed by a procession of op-eds railing against Science Studies. Science Studies was portrayed as but the latest in a series of assaults on reason in higher education. Dubbed "the Science Wars" after the Culture Wars of the 1980s, the hullabaloo spilled into several science-advocacy conferences. *Higher Superstition* and like-minded commentaries also prompted the defensive disparagement of the science defenders by humanities scholars. In the October 2, 1995 issue of *The Nation*, NYU Critical Theory professor Andrew Ross reported on the science advocacy conference sponsored by the New York Academy of Sciences called "The Flight from Science and Reason." Ross dismissed the conference speakers' attacks on Science Studies. He demeaned the science boosters by calling them "Science Warriors," mere carnival barkers of science conservativism. According to Ross, the Science Warriors mischaracterized Science Studies as "anti-Enlightenment irrationalism" and caricatured Science Studies scholars as "boffo nihilists who deny outright the existence of natural phenomena like recessive genes or subatomic particles or even the law of gravity." Ross's remark about Science Studies scholars denying the law of gravity inadvertently portended one of the most remarkable cases of eating crow in modern academic history: the Sokal Hoax.

When NYU physicist Alan Sokal submitted a parody to *Social Text*, a respected Critical Theory and Cultural Studies periodical, the editors, including Ross and City University of New York (CUNY) professor Stanley Aronowitz, ran the piece in a special "Science Wars" spring/summer issue in 1996. Sokal's "Transgressing the Boundaries: Towards a Transformative Hermeneutics of Quantum Gravity" was the final article in the issue. It followed chapters from a star-studded cast of Science Studies scholars. Sokal demonstrated as possible exactly what Ross had dismissed as preposterous – that Science Studies might go so far as to deny the reality of gravity. Sokal managed to put the hoax past Ross himself, who had so recently denied the prospect as outrageous.

"Transgressing the Boundaries" suggested that quantum gravity is a social and linguistic construct and that one could understand quantum mechanics with postmodern theory. Sokal satirically criticized his fellow scientists, because they accepted "the dogma imposed by the long post-Enlightenment hegemony over the Western intellectual outlook: *that there exists an external world*, whose properties are independent of any individual human being and indeed of humanity as a whole." In quantum gravity, "the space-time manifold ceases to exist as an objective physical reality" and "*existence itself become[s] problematized* and relativized" (my emphasis). Littered with jargon and excessive citations of postmodern theorists and signaling radical relativism and extreme skepticism with every turn of phrase, Sokal's essay mimicked Science Studies so successfully that even given the knowledge of the hoax, I wasn't sure just where it merely strained credulity as opposed to being patently ridiculous. Sokal had seamlessly blended the patently ridiculous with the semi-plausible.

The preposterous, satirical claims in Sokal's parody bear an unmistakable likeness to social justice statements, especially in transgender theory. The non-existence, disappearance, or insignificance of physical reality or the external world in Sokal's piece anticipates the transgender belief that the facts of biology have nothing to do with the "reality" of gender identity.

In a subsequent issue of *Lingua Franca* devoted to the Science Wars, Sokal triumphantly spilled the beans. He announced that he had duped the editors of *Social Text* and therefore the entire field of Science Studies. In response, Ross and Columbia University professor of literature Bruce Robbins insisted that Sokal's deception was a serious breach of ethics (as if postmodern Science Studies itself wasn't already an ethical breach). In an attempt to save face, Ross and Robbins suggested that the editorial board had not been utterly bamboozled. They knew the article represented a bad case of mimicry. "From the first, we considered Sokal's unsolicited article to be a little hokey," they wrote.

Yet the title of the article crystalized the significance of the hoax. Postmodern Science Studies had transgressed the boundaries of evidence and rationality and Sokal transgressed the otherwise secure boundaries of Science Studies' hallowed nonsense.

Curiously, although the Science Wars and the Sokal Hoax had been the rage just the year before, Sharon made no mention of it during the semester-long course and no one brought it up. But I taught the controversy in my class, a first-year writing offering entitled "Science, Technology and Society" (STS). Readings included a chapter from Gross and Levitt, along with the some of the material that they and Sokal assailed. My syllabus stacked the deck against the science boosters, suggesting that they erected straw men in place of actual Science Studies criticisms. This was the approach most prominent Science Studies defenders took as well. Sensing that the entire postmodern theoretical enterprise had been exposed by Sokal, even the high-profile literary and legal scholar Stanley Fish attempted a rescue mission. Fish, who had nothing to do with the field of Science Studies, scolded Sokal in the *New York Times* for intellectual dishonesty, while belittling him for misstating the claims and aims of the theoretical field ("Professor Sokal's Bad Joke," May 21, 1996).

After the spring 1998 semester, a student of mine commented on RateMyProfessors.com about my STS course: "A nice enough guy; get to know him. But the subject he teaches – 'Science Studies,' or the sociology of science – is ridiculous and boring. Lots of very difficult readings ..." Looking back, I realize that foisting such hyper-skeptical criticisms of science on first-year students was ethically and intellectually wrong-headed. Science Studies is too insular, peculiar, and fueled by resentment to make sense to early undergraduates. Students beginning their studies in engineering, computer science, theater, math, the sciences, and even humanities should be spared such academic sniping. A first-year student should be invited to appreciate the elegance and accomplishments of their prospective field – at least before being encouraged to disembowel it.

MODERATE VS. RADICAL CONSTRUCTIVISM: REALISM OR MAKE-BELIEVE

Nevertheless, Science Studies became my broad theoretical framework – although not until I had flushed down the drain the worst examples of "cutting-edge" postmodern drivel but also such "backward" perspectives as "naïve empiricism" and Logical Positivism. Empiricism and Logical Positivism were not considered viable as theoretical paradigms within contemporary Science Studies – except as objects of criticism or derision. The more sophisticated Logical Positivism held that scientific theories derive from induction – or the collection of empirical observations from which scientists generalized. From a contemporary Science Studies perspective, Positivism naively placed scientific rationality and empirical observation beyond the reach of society and culture. It thus represented an insularity that was no longer acceptable. The trend was to consider all knowledge claims, including those of science, as driven by social and political interests. Since the knowledge claims of Critical

Theory, Cultural Studies, and postmodern theory were admittedly political, these academic leftists apparently found it impossible to believe
that that the same was not true of every discipline.

In 1976, the Edinburgh sociologist David Bloor introduced the
"Strong Programme" in the *Sociology of Scientific Knowledge* (SSK). Em-
boldened by Thomas Kuhn's notion of the paradigm shift and drawing
from an earlier tradition in the sociology of knowledge, Bloor proposed
that sociologists could examine science for evidence of social causation.
By calling his school of sociology the Strong Programme, Bloor meant
that sociology should aim to breach the very content of science rather than merely explaining extrinsic factors like the speed of research
or amounts of funding, and so forth. Bloor suggested that all scientific
claims, whether tried and true or utterly discredited, should be studied for social causality because social factors act indiscriminately. Since
SSK supposedly withheld judgment regarding the veracity of scientific
claims, it was dubbed a form of epistemological agnosticism, although
most philosophers of science disagreed with the label. They argued that
SSK's inclusion of social causes for true as well as false scientific claims
meant that it took an epistemological stand. If true scientific knowledge
could be caused by social factors then a strict correspondence between
scientific knowledge and the objects of said knowledge was impossible.
Evidence of social causation at the heart of science would mean that
science is adulterated, although Bloor argued that social influence didn't
imply a taint.

SSK has often been regarded as a form of "social constructivism"
or "social and linguistic constructivism." In Science Studies, social and
linguistic constructivism refers to the way social factors shape science,
as well as to the sense that science is ultimately linguistic or symbolic.
The "social" refers to importance of collective belief and the "linguistic"
to the dependence of scientific expression on language or other symbolic systems.

But constructivism may also suggest that scientists create and impose their own (subjective) constructs on the object world rather than
explaining what's actually there. An extreme form known as "radical
constructivism" amounts to social and philosophical idealism or the
perspective that material reality does not significantly constrain our
sensory observations and likewise does not seriously constrain theory
choices. Likewise, one theory is as good as any other for describing the
relevant phenomena. Scientific theories exist in scientists' heads and do
not necessarily correspond to the objects in question.

As I discuss in Chapter 10, radical constructivism can be found in the social justice movement, particularly in transgender theory. Transgender theory holds that empirical data – chromosomes, anatomy, physiology, and hormones – do not determine gender. Gender is determined by beliefs about empirical information, and ultimately, by naming, by language.

Despite the deserved derision directed at the most egregious examples of drivel in Science Studies, I found an approach that I considered credible and coherent. In *Science Studies, An Advanced Introduction* (1997), David Hess introduced the term "moderate constructivism" to describe a social and scientific realism. According to this double realism, science develops more or less accurate maps of its objects of study. At the same time, theories and other scientific activity also reflect the social and cultural contexts of their production. Although the mind-as-mirror metaphor was rejected by the postmodern philosopher Richard Rorty, one might say that science is like a two-sided mirror. One side reflects its natural objects – to greater or lesser degrees of accuracy – while the other reflects its cultural and social provenance. Thus, contrary to radical constructivism, science certainly does tell us something about nature. But contrary to Logical Positivism, it also tells us something about culture and society as well.

For example, without calling into question the truth status of Darwinian evolutionary theory, one might nevertheless note that Darwin's idea of natural selection (and the origin of species) became possible only upon the rise of modern industrial capitalism. Before the nineteenth century, social mobility was uncommon. In the feudal period, the cosmological order was conceived of as a Great Chain of Being, a fixed hierarchy with God at the apex, descending through the angels, including humanity and the ranking within the social order, and continuing through the entire animal and plant kingdoms, to inanimate matter. The Great Chain of Being was represented by Alexander Pope in his philosophical poem, *Essay on Man* (1734):

> See, through this air, this ocean, and this earth,
> All matter quick, and bursting into birth.
> Above, how high, progressive life may go!
> Around, how wide! how deep extend below?
> Vast chain of being! which from God began,
> Natures ethereal, human, angel, man,
> Beast, bird, fish, insect, what no eye can see,

No glass can reach; from Infinite to thee,
From thee to nothing.

With the social mobility made possible under industrial capitalism, a rising industrial ownership class challenged the aristocracy for
dominance. At the same time, many workers, who had been independent producers in cottage industries, were driven to the factories and
the cities, and in many cases, into privation. The stasis of the social order
was upended. Arguably, the social mobility of the industrial revolution
made possible Darwin's vision of the shifting fortunes of individuals,
varieties, and species in nature.

ACADEMIC PROPAGANDA AND AN ANTIDOTE

In broader terms, I worked within a subfield of literary studies
called Science and Literature Studies (SLS). Initiated by Victorian literary scholars Gillian Beer and George Levine, at its best, this subfield of
English Studies involved examining the shared cultural bases for science
and literature so that commonly held goals, myths, narratives, and plots
might be explored and explained. At its worst, scholars in the subfield
merely tracked the literary elements in science and the scientific elements in literature, as if mere sharing explained anything at all. In my
cultural period exam essay, I argued for a revision of the subfield after
a model that I borrowed from Michel Foucault's *The Order of Things*
(1956). More than merely interacting dialectically, science and culture
were mutually affected by a third element – an episteme running like
ground water beneath and between both. I had pursued this line of
thinking in an essay on science and culture in George Eliot's novel *Middlemarch.*

After lighting upon the conjuncture of nineteenth-century British
science and culture, I couldn't let it go. I was enraptured. For example,
the theoretical battles between vitalism and materialism in the early
1820s, between "catastrophism" and "uniformitarianism" in the early
1830s and between natural theology and scientific naturalism from the
1850s on intrigued me to no end. My mentor was Assistant Professor
Gary Willingham-McClain. His dissertation had been about the organ-
ic, scientific sublime or the overwhelming plenum of ecological complexity that he saw in the works of Darwin and George Eliot. Gary left
after my second year to become a Protestant seminarian. Before he quit,
he confessed to me that he'd been a covert Biblical literalist hiding out in

a Cultural Studies department for five years. But he was also a Marxist. He married Marxism and Biblical literalism by virtue of some intellectual gymnastics, claiming that Marxism was a methodological materialism rather than a philosophical materialism – that is, that it limited itself to the treatment of the material realm, without asserting anything about the supra-material or supernatural. He believed that Marxism did not foreclose a belief in God. Of course, this is belied by the evidence of Marx's own writing. But Gary believed that Marxism expressed the truth about human material (in)justice on earth, while Christianity expressed the truth about ultimate human purpose and destiny in heaven. To replace Gary, the department hired Jon Klancher, a seasoned, no-nonsense and very narrowly academic new historicist. Jon was skeptical of Science Studies and my project at first, but soon came around to my way of seeing things.

I was drawn more by the science than the literature element of the science and literature equation, and to the history of science itself – not only because I loved science but also due to the anxiety I felt regarding the state of literary studies in English. As I saw it, very little that passed for research amounted to worthy scholarship. Most of it struck me not only as politically motivated but also as sheer propaganda – although a very sophisticated type of propaganda – academic propaganda. Scholars regularly treated literary texts as palimpsests for drawing, willy-nilly, whatever conclusions they wanted to draw from them. They admittedly projected their contemporary pet obsessions onto literary texts in deliberate and sometimes ludicrous ways. Literary and other texts served as mere props, grounds for advancing an agenda, usually one having to do with a "radical" identity. Queer theorists, for example, explicitly seek to "queer the text," to make it bend over to the demands of a queer reading. I wasn't interested – not primarily because I didn't "identify as" queer but because I didn't accept such blatantly political approaches to literary or historical studies. Such "specialists" used the field to advance their identity politics agendas, while cashing in on their special snowflake identities to advance their careers. And none dared question this hijacking of the profession – lest he be called a homophobe, sexist, transphobe, or worse, a mere curmudgeon.

The history of science was my antidote to such academic propaganda. I studied the history of chemistry, geology, and evolution and defined my "cultural object" as nineteenth-century scientific materialism – an episteme underlying several revolutions in the sciences and evident in various cultural, social, and political domains. I was not content with melting-down the coinage of science into the base metal of "mere language" – like so many postmodern Science Studies practitioners were wont to do. I sought to understand the actual content and historical significance of the sciences, as well as grappling with what I termed "the extra-scientific signs of science"– the marks of beliefs deemed "scientific" on broader cultural, political, and social domains.

POSTMODERN SUICIDE

After three years in the program, I had finished my classwork and qualifying exams and worked full-time as a writer in an Artificial Intelligence lab of CMU's Robotics Institute, while also writing a dissertation and teaching classes at two different universities. Then "the unthinkable" happened. An email alert announced attacks on the World Trade Center. I rushed to the lounge of the lab to follow the TV coverage.

Not long after 9/11, academics began to weigh in on its cultural and political meanings (or lack thereof). Ward Churchill's scandalous reference to the victims of 9/11 as "little Eichmanns" provided fodder for political talk-show outrage. On the other hand, Jean Baudrillard contributed the quintessential postmodern response, which went largely unremarked upon outside of academia. In *Simulations* (1983), Baudrillard had described the postmodern world as a series of simulacra, a spectacle of simulations without originals. Suburban neighborhoods, amusement parks, jungle dioramas in shopping malls, and even the political left and right – these were all simulations without originals, imitations without prototypes. Baudrillard enraged both left and right when he remarked that the first Gulf War "wasn't real." He meant that the real had been displaced by images and history by the serial reproduction of imagery.

The Twin Towers were also simulacra, doubled apparitions of the digital core of monopoly capitalism. The twins stood for monopoly in the sense that their "identicality" (Urban Dictionary) meant that competition had been eliminated. "Perfect parallelepipeds," Baudrillard wrote, the Twin Towers represented duplication but also duplicity – their sameness revealing the false singularity of reproductions, the absence of originals.

Baudrillard didn't describe the attacks on the World Trade Center as a mere simulation, however. Although he stated that 9/11's symbolic resonance outweighed its "real" impact, Baudrillard saw 9/11 as a resuscitation of the real, if only in terrorism. Like 9/11 conspiracy theorists, he rejected the "official narrative." But unlike 9/11 "truthers," Baudrillard did not propose an alternate grand narrative. Rather, he viewed the remains of the Twin Towers as he did the world – as the fragmented semblance of a reality that could never be reconstructed in a way that made sense. The postmodern is a constructed and tragically-ironically-named "Freedom Tower" that has displaced the real. As a scavenger expelled from reality, the postmodern theorist feasted on the discovery of reality's dead corpse with a *jouissance* that only a terrorist could relish in such a meal.

Rather than "an inside job," Baudrillard suggested that 9/11 represented a suicide, self-destruction committed by everyone within the global system. The self-immolation hadn't been planned so much as wished for – by everyone, including its victims. According to Baudrillard, everyone who witnessed "the event" openly or secretly rejoiced at the exposure of weakness at the epicenter of power. "The moral condemnation and the holy alliance against terrorism are on the same scale as the prodigious jubilation at seeing this global superpower destroyed – better, at seeing it, in a sense, destroying itself, committing suicide." Even those who enjoyed its advantages held a death wish for the global system's uncontested power. Even its victims had been "complicit" in the system's symbolic demise. The West acted the part of "accomplice in its own destruction."

While including recommendations for containing the viral infiltration of terrorism, Baudrillard's sympathetic understanding of the insidious Other registered a certain malevolence. In his theoretical enthusiasm, Baudrillard not only evinced a death wish for the Western world but also betrayed moral nihilism and a cultivated indifference to the reality of mass murder. His 9/11 meditations thus stand as an indictment of the postmodern theoretical project itself: a postmodern theoretical suicide.

CHAPTER 7

ACADEMIC LEFTISM AND THE ABOLITION OF THE FAMILY

THE KIND OF MAN I ADMIRE

I N THE *Manifesto of the Communist Party* of 1848, Karl Marx and Friedrich Engels wrote that the modern family was a product and function of capitalism. They suggested that the bourgeois family, the family of the capitalist class, was based strictly "on capital, on private gain." On the other hand, among the working class, the family did not exist: "But this state of things finds its complement in the practical absence of the family among the proletarians, and in public prostitution." They continued: "The bourgeois family will vanish as a matter of course when its complement [the proletariat] vanishes, and both will vanish with the vanishing of capital."

As I was wont to do, I saw this passage not only as a diagnosis of capitalism and a prognosis for socialism but also as symptomatic of my personal and family circumstances. Changing careers in my early thirties to begin a long academic apprenticeship put my relationship with Gretchen under considerable stress, and also jeopardized our family life. The time I spent taking classes, reading, writing, and finally mounting the dissertation not only cut deeply into our time together but more significantly my obsession with the field drove us apart.

Gretchen worked in low-income property management and my rather arcane pursuits were growing more and more remote from her interests and knowledge base. When we met for lunch one weekday, I felt like I was talking to a veritable stranger. She wore a shirt with a company logo, which I found sad. Other than our children and home, as became clear during that off-site meeting, we no longer had much in common. She wanted to continue the marital and family life, which seemed to be slipping away from her. I was so obsessed with my Ph.D. studies that I lost track of other values. She had no interest in my studies and once mocked my interests: "Who cares about Victorian poetry?" I was particularly interested in Victorian science, not so much Victorian poetry, although I loved Tennyson. Her "mistake" showed just how far we had drifted apart.

One day I came home to find my books gone from the French cabinets in the living room and office. When I asked where they were, Gretchen said that she had boxed and stowed them in an upstairs closet. I went to retrieve the books and found that they had been thrown into the boxes, apparently with little regard. They were half-open, dog-eared, and interleaved with each other.

On vacation at Rehoboth Beach during the summer of 2001, our marital crisis crystalized in a short exchange. As the kids swam and made sandcastles, Gretchen and I enjoyed our favorite pastime – reading on the beach. Once again, books were the focus of contention. Gretchen read *Seabiscuit: The True Story of Three Men and a Racehorse*, by Laura Hillenbrand, while I read *Victorian Infidels: The Origins of the British Secularist Movement 1791-1866*, by Edward Royle. (Although at the time, I felt lightyears from a career in the field and never imagined writing a book on par with Royle's, years later I saw the publication of my book, *Nineteenth-Century British Secularism: Science, Religion, and Literature* (2016), which drew an email from Royle, who mostly praised it and defended his work from the criticisms that my book included.)

After an hour or so, Gretchen looked up from her book and declared:

"See, this is the kind of man I admire!" – referring to the businessman, the horse-trading Charles Howard, one of the book's three heroes.

"I think we have a problem," I answered.

By no means did I mean to suggest that my pursuits were better than those of a horse trader. Nor did I wish to denigrate her reading diet. I simply pointed to an obvious conflict and growing incompatibility. While I had once been the wheeling-and-dealing businessman she still related to, I could never be him, again.

THE DANCER FROM THE DANCE

By the spring of 2003, I had separated from Gretchen and was living in a house only a few blocks from the family home. At the suggestion of my therapist, I joined one of his group therapy cohorts. It was during one of these sessions that I first saw Sarah.

On her first session with the group, we formed a circle as usual. Sarah and I sat directly opposite each other. I tried to gander at her as often and inconspicuously as possible. She had straight black hair and sharp facial features, with especially high cheekbones. She wore cut-off jeans revealing knobby knees. Her humble-bragging confessions of artistic doubt, and her knobby knees, enchanted me. The former indicated vulnerability and the latter a mild imperfection that rendered her approachable, yet somehow more attractive. For some incomprehensible reason, I took both as signs of our fateful connection.

After two group sessions, I worked up the nerve to ask Sarah out. I approached her as she was unlocking her bicycle from a pole and started a conversation about the group discussion. Within a minute, I hurriedly asked if she wanted to grab a bite to eat, so that we could continue talking more comfortably.

"Sure," she answered, agreeably. Her snappy decision suggested that she'd expected such a proposition from me, had already decided to say yes, and had been waiting for me to get around to asking. However, we were overheard by another group member. Chip, a leather-clad motorcyclist with a pock-marked face, asked if he could join us.

Without hesitation, but with a marked lack of enthusiasm, we both said "sure." Saying "no" to this request was impossible at this point. It would have betrayed and risked undermining any romantic intentions in play. The three of us agreed to meet directly after at Thai Place in Shadyside.

Sarah talked about her career and status as a well-known New York choreographer. She was visiting Pittsburgh as an artist-in-residence at the Andy Warhol Museum on the North Side, the part of town where I'd grown up. She looked toward me as if suggesting that I reciprocate and talk about my career.

I started to describe my field, which was now called "Literary and Cultural Studies" (the department having changed its name from Literary and Cultural Theory). As I routinely did when explaining it to lay people, I agonized over what "literary and cultural studies" meant. "Literary studies" was not what happened in English departments of yore, and "cultural studies" was not what it seemed to suggest either – as it did for me at first, something like cultural anthropology.

Chip then chipped in, as if answering a question. He announced that he was the Director of Water Quality and Production for the City of Pittsburgh. He clearly attempted to compete with me for Sarah's attention. His opening gambit consisted of mentioning a few recherché water purification tidbits, simultaneously demonstrating his professional superiority over me, as well as his clearly more peculiar and zany intellect. Ignoring Chip, Sarah uttered the words "cultural studies," enunciating the phrase playfully but also with a peculiar emphasis indicative of knowing what she was talking about.

She even mentioned one its leading lights: "Michel Foucault!"

I felt sorry for Chip but also wanted him gone. Surely, he must have recognized what an awkward position he occupied as a third-wheel in a conversation that sought to exclude him.

Sarah asked whether I dealt with this theorist. I was in the late stages of writing a dissertation on what I called "the publics of science," in which I located politically-motivated science cultures surrounding nineteenth-century British periodicals. While I drew slightly from Adorno, Lukács, Foucault, and others, the theorists that mattered most to my project were those from the sociology of scientific knowledge: Barry Barnes, David Bloor, Bruno Latour, and others. Jürgen Habermas's treatment of the "public sphere" also made him central. A few philosophers of science came in for discussion: Karl Popper, Thomas Kuhn, Steve Fuller, and others.

She was duly impressed.

Chip leaned forward. He remarked that the water quality in New York was much better than most people thought. I politely asked about the safety of chemical additives.

"They evaporate after a few hours of exposure to the air," he explained.

"Oh," I said, trying to feign the slightest interest.

Sarah and I continued our conspicuous signaling of mutual attraction. In fact, Chip's efforts only underscored our obvious flirtation and courtship. His weak efforts to participate in the conversation served as a foil for the rapport that clearly existed between Sarah and me.

After dinner, as Sarah unlocked her bicycle from a telephone poll, she looked up to me and said softly, "Goodbye Michael." I knew for certain that this salutation was not final. Her careful naming of me was a kind of love-making; she formed my name in her mouth and issued it forth with care, delivering me to myself.

After that first date, Sarah and I finally met alone for coffee at a Starbucks in Squirrel Hill. I told her about my apprenticeship with Allen Ginsberg, my subsequent work in advertising, and my later return to graduate school. She talked about her choreography. I mentioned that I'd done some research on her and that I was impressed.

It was then that I noticed her thumbnails. She apparently bit them as vigorously I did my baby fingernails. I brought our mutual self-mutilation to her attention. Soon, we would acknowledge this peculiar similarity as a sign of compatibility – even of inevitable connection. It was a shared addiction – one among others.

On the Friday night of the next week, we drove in my van to a club in Monroeville to hear a friend's band play. She began complaining about "the suburbs." I thought this indicated immaturity, snobbery, or both. Suddenly embarrassed about driving this sophisticate in a soccer dad's minivan to a suburban Pittsburgh nightclub, I declared that I despised the notion that New York was deemed the only place in America where an artist or intellectual could possibly thrive.

After that night, I lost track of her. Her six-week artist-in-residence stint neared its end and her return to New York was imminent. For some reason, I had made no plans with her. I even failed to ask for an email address or phone number. Yet from her schedule with the Warhol and her mention of leaving the very day after finishing the residency, I figured out her departure date.

On the Sunday that she was due to leave, I drove to the house where she'd stayed in Shadyside. Racing the van from Point Breeze, I heard a flapping, thumping sound. In the right lane of Fifth Avenue, I jacked up the right front of the van, unscrewed the bolts, and replaced the flat tire with the undersized spare. By then it was late afternoon and my hands were covered in grease. I raced to the door of the house where Sarah had stayed. The romanticism of the situation was not lost on me. I played a part in a movie and this was one of the most gripping scenes. I knocked. I rang the bell. I repeated, again and again. No one answered. She was gone.

The next morning, I sat in my office, despairing. Had I really let her slip away?

But by 9 AM, miraculously, I received an email from her – a chipper and fetching communiqué. It was still on. From that point, the connection was never to be risked again by indolence on my part or impudence on hers. Our exchanges were constant, intense, and extremely exciting. They brought her back to Pittsburgh for visits in no time and took me to New York as well.

There are many salient episodes in the romance that I might add. I'll mention only a few here. One was the time we were spiritually "married" (after I'd filed for divorce from Gretchen) during an Easter Sunday service at Grace Episcopal Church on Broadway in Noho, when we experienced collectively and individually what we both described as the kneading together of our souls. Another was a dance performance in Union Square. The "dance" happened above us on ropes. After craning our necks for an hour, our heads released from their upward gazes, and we turned toward each other and kissed. Once on a bus from Soho to Tribeca, Sarah gently laid her head on my shoulder.

Over the next few weeks, I implored Sarah to leave her beloved New York and to move into the Point Breeze house in Pittsburgh I'd recently bought. She soon obliged.

Almost a year later, in early 2006, Sarah decided to undertake a year-long, low-residency M.F.A. in dance at Hollins University in western Virginia. I supposed that she now aspired, like me (and perhaps due to some implicit suggestion of mine), to become an academic. She went, leaving me for the longest stretch I'd experienced on my own in many years. Feelings of long-familiar but rarely felt abandonment bubbled up like forgotten childhood acquaintances.

CHAPTER 8
DUKING IT OUT AT NCCU

"THE DUKE LACROSSE RAPE CASE"

I N THE SPRING OF 2006, I was invited to interview for a tenure-track job at North Carolina Central University (NCCU) in Durham. I accepted the interview and began preparations.

I had recently received other offers, but none was for a tenure-track position. One was from Georgia Tech, to become a postdoctoral fellow in digital theory. As a digital theory postdoc, I would participate in seminars on digital theory and pedagogy, studying under the supervision and mentorship of the ground-breaking and celebrated digital media theorist, Jay Bolter. I would teach three classes per year, of my own design. West Virginia University offered me a non-tenure-track position as an instructor teaching three courses per semester. Another possibility was to stay at CMU, spending another year as a postdoc.

After applying for nearly a hundred jobs that year, the interview at NCCU looked like the last chance for a tenure-track offer. After a phone interview with the department chair, I had had a strong feeling that I could win the position.

There was a wrinkle, however, and the wrinkle looked like it might point to a deeper fault line. The interview was scheduled to take place in the midst of a national media frenzy over the alleged rape of a black woman by members of the Duke lacrosse team. The story was regularly referred to as "the Duke lacrosse rape case." I had followed it closely and it looked very bad for the players involved. A lesser-known detail about the case was that the alleged victim had been an NCCU student. I knew this and probably most of the details that possibly could be known by a non-participant.

NCCU was one of a number of the country's historically black colleges and universities (HBCUs). The university had a predominantly black student population and a significant contingent of black faculty members. Looking forward to the interview, as a white man, I felt uncomfortable about the prospect of answering questions about the alleged rape case involving a gang of white men and a black woman. I worried about where such questioning might lead.

In fact, I had slight misgivings about presenting my qualifications for teaching at an HBCU in the first place – especially to black faculty members. The chair of the department was white, and during our one-on-one phone interview, she seemed to have gone so far as to apologize for the fact that the job entailed teaching mostly black students. This made me uncomfortable at the time and whenever I thought about it. Surely this was not a representative attitude among the faculty? But what might I expect? Wouldn't overt hostility be among the possibilities?

I asked Jon Klancher, my dissertation advisor, how to handle the rape allegation controversy during the interview, should it come up. I imagined it very well might. What should I say if asked about it? I wondered.

Jon's advice was a bit comical as I came to see it later. He advised me to pretend that I hadn't heard about the case at all. I should say that I knew nothing about it. Just deny any knowledge about it. That would immunize me entirely.

How could I possibly claim that? He said to tell them that I was one of those academic types who didn't pay attention to mass media, whose academic interests kept them so busy and engaged that they didn't bother to follow the news. I buried my head in my research and never watched TV and didn't even read the papers.

In this particular instance, I didn't find Jon's advice at all helpful, although he'd been brilliant about many other professional concerns. First of all, I was precisely not that kind of academic, and I didn't think I could successfully pretend to be. At this point, I saw myself as politically engaged and viewed my academic work as part of a cultural politics.

Plus, anyone who Googled my name might see that I was a minor media pundit. I'd appeared numerous times on MSNBC TV, usually on "Scarborough Country," a nightly political talking-head show hosted by Joe Scarborough, and broadcast before MSNBC "leaned forward" – that is, before it was recognized as the so-called left-leaning network that it is today. At the time, Joe Scarborough was (or pretended to be) much further to the right than he is (or pretends to be) today. I was regularly brought on as a standard liberal punching bag. One night, after I declared on national TV that I thought George W. Bush was a war criminal, Scarborough even went so far as to suggest that I might rightfully be charged with treason. I was not sure whether this suggestion was part of an acting stunt on Scarborough's part, or whether he meant it. I had a feeling that it was an act, however. In fact, I had a sense that all of the political talk shows were analogous to studio wrestling; they involved staged, faux conflicts. On a night that I was set to face off with Ann Coulter, I heard her talking on a hot microphone before airtime. She heaped praise on me, speaking highly of "that Rectenwald guy," saying "I love him!" She advocated that I be brought on more often. Why would she applaud a left-liberal if she truly despised leftists and liberals, I thought – unless, that is, she really didn't?

Further, if I pretended to be such an aloof scholar during the interview, how could I simultaneously claim to be prepared or sufficiently engaged to teach historically and economically disadvantaged students, such as those who attended NCCU? I decided that if asked about the case, I would lament the situation, express my deep empathy for the alleged victim, and point to my own quite visible historical support for the disadvantaged and oppressed. That was the best way to go, I thought.

During the interview, I read from a dissertation chapter that dealt with working-class intellectuals, and after this short exhibition, I stressed once more my commitment to working-class education and working-class students. I didn't use the word "race." I sensed "epistemic pushback" from a few African-American women in the room. They were attending faculty members, but none of them were on the hiring committee.

"How would you teach an African-American student?" one of them asked.

I was momentarily nonplussed and had to pause briefly. My unfettered impulse would have been to answer, "just as I would any other student." What other response could possibly be acceptable? The question implied an essentialism about African Americans, something about their essence that I as a white person did not share and could not possibly grasp. Such essentialism had been a theoretical basis for racism. Another plausible interpretation was that being black in America represented circumstances that a white person had never experienced and therefore could not understand. The gulf between whites and blacks was thus unbridgeable. As such, a white teacher could not effectively teach a black student. I didn't like the implications in either case. I rejected an essential difference between racial groups. Anyway, couldn't one human being empathize with another, even if their identities and circumstances varied widely? If not, what hope could there be to overcome issues like racism and economic disadvantage? Didn't the imagination allow for sympathy and wasn't sympathy the basis of morality, as Shelley had argued in *A Defence of Poetry*?

I side-stepped the question a bit by referring to my own working-class background and the struggles that I had encountered as I labored to become an intellectual and an academic from such a starting point. That is, I disavowed the first plausible interpretation of the question and tried to breach the gulf represented by the second. But I knew I needed to say more – particularly in connection with the implications about racism and racist oppression. I suggested that the abolitionist and Civil Rights movements demonstrated that the human capacity for empathy was sufficiently strong to allow people to imagine themselves in the position of others, and in some limited yet profound sense, to feel their feelings. This same sympathetic sense formed the basis for effective communications and teaching. And both professors and students had things they could teach and learn from each other.

I was satisfied that I really could do no better than this and in fact that perhaps nothing better could be done. No one asked about "the Duke lacrosse rape case" and I surely wasn't about to bring it up. Thus, I managed to come away from the interview relatively unscathed.

The next day, I received a call from the department chair, offering me the job. I asked for a couple days to decide.

AN IDYLLIC COLLEGE CAMPUS

I weighed my options: Georgia Tech, West Virginia, CMU, NCCU. Although it was a paid, three-year position and included benefits, and although the opportunity to work with Bolter proved attractive, the position at Georgia Tech essentially represented an extension of my already overlong apprenticeship. It also involved increasing the risk of age discrimination when I faced the job market again in three years. I was already forty-four. Besides, the salary was unlivable for a person with three children. The West Virginia offer was for a low-pay, no future job. The only advantage it presented was that I could remain close to home and could spend weekends in Pittsburgh. Staying at CMU meant getting nowhere. Finally, every reputable academic I asked stated unequivocally that any tenure-track job was preferable to any non-tenure-track job, period. Even a professor at Georgia Tech told me this, while stressing how much they would love to have me there.

I was very much swayed by the advice of professionals and leaned toward accepting the NCCU offer. And there was yet another factor – and it cinched my decision. Sarah's MFA program would soon take her to Durham and Duke University, the home of the American Dance Festival. So, when at last I moved there, Sarah and I were back together, this time in a spacious loft adjacent to Duke's East Campus. Sarah then told me of a dream she had while she still lived in New York, soon after we'd met. In her dream, she and I walked together through an idyllic college campus, in our new world together.

The NCCU job was far from ideal. The teaching load was quite heavy – a "four-four" load, or four courses per semester. NCCU was a poor, apparently neglected cousin within the University of North Carolina (UNC) system. Although boasting of its proximity to the Research Triangle, the campus itself was discouraging. Many buildings were run-down, the library collection was meagre at best, most of the computers in the labs did not work or ran slowly, and even the food selection on campus was terrible. The only vendor of prepared foods in the student union was Kentucky Fried Chicken. Academically, the school was ranked very low, even among third-tier schools. Admitted students presented some of the lowest average SAT scores of any college or university in the country, and the lowest in the UNC system.

I had to be a jack of all trades at NCCU. I taught first-year writing, technical writing, web writing, interpreting literature, and world literature. I was asked to develop and implement core courses for a new writing concentration, including designing two keystone courses, which I called Writing for Science and Technology and Writing for Digital Media.

To make matters even more interesting, I decided to email the Director of the Writing Program at Duke, Joe Harris, to ask if he might have an interest in my teaching first-year writing there. I wanted to teach at Duke not only because it was such a high-profile institution but also because I wanted to keep my intellectual identity alive. I feared going under at NCCU, never to be heard from again.

After brushing me off at first, Joe wrote a second time and asked to meet me at his office. We got along swimmingly. My pedagogical training in first-year writing at CMU put me in good stead with him and we seemed to like each other personally. So, by my first spring semester at

NCCU, I was also teaching a course at Duke. My course, an adaptation of the first-year seminar syllabus that Martha Woodmansee shared with me, was called "Creativity and Property." It explored the eighteenth-century and nineteenth-century roots of modern authorship and intellectual property and their impact on literature, the sciences and technology, and world cultures.

A WAC INITIATIVE

As if I didn't have enough to do, early in the fall of 2007, I had an idea for building a curricular bridge between Duke and NCCU. The idea was for a collaborative project involving Duke's Writing Program and NCCU's writing-across-the-curriculum (WAC) initiative. I talked to Joe Harris about it. As Joe and I began to articulate it together, the project would involve pairing Duke University Writing Fellows – who held the Ph.D. in various disciplines – with NCCU faculty in the sciences, social sciences, arts, and humanities. As we envisioned it, the Duke Writing Fellows would assist the participating NCCU faculty with writing-intensive courses in their respective disciplines. Both institutions stood to benefit. The Duke writing fellows stood to gain teaching experience outside of the elite Duke demographic, a demographic in which few would ever land tenure-track jobs. NCCU's fledgling WAC initiative would benefit from the assistance of the Duke fellows. Moreover, the project might even help to improve historically fraught relations between these neighboring institutions, strained relations that had recently been exacerbated by "the Duke lacrosse rape case."

After my meeting with Joe, I mentioned the idea to Louise Maynor, my department chair at NCCU. Then, it began to gain legs. A meeting of faculty from both institutions was scheduled. The meeting included five faculty members from NCCU and two from Duke. While we were seating ourselves, most of us made friendly small talk. But my NCCU colleague Karen Jackson insisted that we begin by "knowing just who we are talking to."

"I'll begin," she said with what appeared to be an inexplicable bitterness. "I am the Director of Writing at North Carolina Central University."

Until then, it I hadn't crossed my mind that by initiating this project, I might have posed a threat to someone's professional identity and status. Karen Jackson had obviously taken umbrage at my audacity. I had introduced a major writing initiative involving NCCU, without consulting her first.

After this meeting, the idea seemed to die a natural death. Then, in the spring of 2008, an email from Karen Jackson to the entire faculty announced, among her other accomplishments, the initiative she had originated for an inter-institutional affiliation with Duke involving their Writing Program Fellows and NCCU's writing-across-the-curriculum faculty participants.

I hadn't been proprietary about academic credit for original ideas – until, that is, I was blatantly robbed. Jackson had surreptitiously buried, then subsequently stolen and taken sole credit for this idea, an idea that one might say was my idea. Yet she was the proprietary one, only the property she claimed wasn't hers.

I called my long-time friend and political associate Lori Price to tell her what happened, knowing she would share my fury. While still on the phone, I attempted to forward the email to her. Above the body of Jackson's email, I wrote: "Here's the email where the bitch takes credit for my ideas!"

Within minutes, I received a private email from Karen Jackson, which included only the following: "Michael?!!!" I thought I was forwarding the email to Lori, but I had mistakenly replied to Karen Jackson instead.

By this point, I had recently received a job offer from NYU, so I wasn't overly concerned about the consequences of my mistaken reply. In any case, I was still angry about the legerdemain on Karen Jackson's part. My mistake was just that: a mistake, not any intentional harm-doing. And although the charge of "racism" was all but inevitable, I knew that racism had nothing to do with what I'd written.

But I was disconcerted when I received a visit from the new chair of the department, Jim Pearce. Jim and I were friends. Over the course of two years, we had talked about many issues, including Barack Obama and his chances for the presidency. Jim thought the Democratic primary represented a set-up, that Obama was chosen in the primaries only to make sure that the Democrats would lose in the general election. He was a lamb for the slaughter, Jim said. I told Jim that I understood his concern. I didn't agree with Jim, but I didn't say so. I thought Obama would actually win the general election. I had heard him speak on campus, and thought I recognized a juggernaut gaining momentum. I didn't like Obama much, for reasons having nothing to do with his race – except that I thought that the use being made of his racial identity was cynical and dishonest. But I couldn't possibly know who was responsible for that. I had been careful not to say anything about it around NCCU.

Jim gently told me what I already knew – calling a black woman a "bitch" was a no-no. Another factor about Karen Jackson must be mentioned. She had only one arm. As such, I had called a one-armed black woman a bitch.

"I hadn't meant for her to see that," I told Jim.

"I know," he said.

"My use of that word had nothing to do with her race. I was infuriated by her dishonesty."

"I know," Jim said.

He then informed me that he would have to put something in my file about the incident. I told him that I understood.

Within a few days, Jim came by my office again, this time to implore me to stay at NCCU. He promised to match NYU's salary offer. But it was too late. I was already gone. I'd accepted NYU's offer and was happy to be headed there. In any case, Sarah had been offered and accepted a job at Dickinson College in Carlisle, PA. The NYU job would put only three hours of driving between us. Remaining at NCCU would mean rarely seeing each other and may have even jeopardized our relationship. (The relationship lasted nine more years but wouldn't endure in the long run, for other reasons. I've been sworn to secrecy about it. But I will say that it had something to do with "social justice.")

As for NCCU, I knew that my difficulty with Karen Jackson represented an underlying and deeper trouble. Long before the incident, and in fact from the outset of my time there, I sensed hostility and resentment directed at me from black faculty members, especially those on contract and with no prospect for tenure. The racial animus combined with the enormous difficulty involved in teaching vastly underprepared students left me exhausted and angry. I felt like I was peeling away layers and layers of social and cultural complexity, which presented an intellectual challenge, but which ultimately left me feeling guilty while being institutionally abused. If I had remained there, I thought, I might never publish a word and would certainly resent the place for draining me of intellectual joy while foreclosing my chances of being an active scholar. Other than my collaboration with my former NCCU colleague Lisa Carl on a Writing Across the Curriculum textbook that we co-authored for publication, I was finished with NCCU.

CHAPTER 9
NYU: ALL THAT SHINES IS NOT GOLD

I LANDED THE JOB in the Liberal Studies Program at NYU. I began in the fall of 2008 and for the first seven years, I was Dean Schwarzbach's golden boy. Within weeks after my arrival at NYU, he selected me to be one of only ten pilot faculty members (from a faculty of over eighty) to lead in the development of a new B.A. program in Global Liberal Studies, a program which promised to offer an innovative B.A. degree for top-notch student prospects. I designed and taught one of the first courses for the new program in my second year at NYU.

I was chosen two years straight to be one of two faculty keynote speakers at Accepted Students Day, charged with delivering a compelling and entertaining presentation to prospective Global Liberal Studies students.

I was chosen to teach at our London campus by my third year. Teaching abroad was an honor and also a significant reward. In London, the position included free housing in a well-appointed apartment building, a light teaching load, and no committee work.

In 2012, I approached Dean Schwarzbach with an idea for an international conference, the first of its kind for Liberal Studies. He approved the request, and in 2013, I chaired the first ever international scholarly conference hosted by the program. I entitled it "Global Secularisms" in keeping with the new global program in Liberal Studies. The conference attracted participants from Belgium, Germany, India, Italy, the Netherlands, Norway, Spain, the UK, the US, and Turkey, and represented numerous universities including the University of Antwerp, Brown University, the University of Chicago, Columbia University, European University Institute, George Washington University, Harvard

University, the University of London, Northwestern University, the University of Oslo, the University of Pittsburgh, Princeton University, Rutgers University, SUNY Binghamton, UC-Davis, and Yale University, as well as New York University. Also represented were the Centre for the study of Developing Societies in India, UNESCO, and One Law for All in Great Britain. An anthology based on the conference, *Global Secularisms in a Post-Secular Age*, which I co-edited with distinguished Victorianist George Levine, appeared in September 2015. Also, in 2013, I founded and edited the first online journal for promoting the accomplishments and undertakings of Liberal Studies faculty.

It was only when my views about social justice ideology became public that I came into conflict with the dean and the entire Liberal Studies faculty of almost one hundred members. But even before the fallout treated in Chapter Two, and in fact as a prelude to it, I had felt the effects of the social justice creed in operation within the program. I will mention one such instance here.

In the fall of 2015, I was appointed by Dean Schwarzbach to serve as the chair for a writing hiring committee, a committee charged with hiring one full-time writing professor. The Liberal Studies program sought someone who could not only teach first-year writing but also offerings in journalism.

The committee of four met in the late fall to discuss the first group of candidates that we had already interviewed in the first round by Skype, before beginning the second set of Skype interviews. In the course of this discussion, I mentioned an email I'd received from one of the candidates from the first Skype batch — let's call the applicant Candidate A. I had forwarded Candidate A's email to the committee. I argued in that email and then in person that the thank-you note sent to me by Candidate A effectively disqualified the applicant. The email was riddled with awkward expression, malapropisms, misplaced punctuation, and other writing problems. I had received emails of similar quality from first-year students, but I surely did not expect to receive such an email from a writing professor, or someone applying to become a writing professor. I asked my three fellow committee members how we could possibly hire someone to teach writing who had written such an email, despite the fact that it represented only a piece of occasional writing. I recalled aloud Candidate A's application letter, which was similarly awkward and error-laden.

"The candidate cannot *write*," I said emphatically. One of the committee colleagues became particularly upset.

"We do not teach grammar!" one committee member insisted.

"But surely a writing professor should know grammar!" I replied.

In the Skype interview following this discussion, the same committee member who had become upset about my remarks regarding Candidate A proceeded to attack another applicant — let's call the applicant Candidate B. In fact, just before the interview, this same colleague, enraged by my criticisms regarding Candidate A, announced that she would ruthlessly attack Candidate B. She did just that. She asked increasingly inappropriate questions and adopted a belligerent tone and aggressive posture. Candidate B, incidentally, had done fascinating scholarship on the late eighteenth-century public sphere, the very birthplace of the field of journalism. The candidate had earned his Ph.D. from a top-ten English department, had since accrued considerable teaching experience in relevant subjects, and presented a record of noteworthy publications, including both academic scholarship and digital journalism. Except when he was being harangued by my militant colleague, Candidate B interviewed very well; the candidate should have been a finalist for the job.

After this disgraceful display of unprofessionalism and blatant bias, I admonished my colleague.

"That was way over-the-top!"

I was then on the receiving end of her verbal barrage. Not only did she pelt me with choice expletives but also, she rose from her chair and posed as if to charge me physically, all the while flailing her limbs and yelling. I immediately left the room and proceeded to the dean's office. I told the dean what had just occurred. He advised me to let it rest until the following week.

What happened next was telling. I found myself enmeshed in an identity politics imbroglio. The colleague who had verbally attacked me was a black female and Candidate A, whom she championed, was also a black female. I was informed by the dean that pursuing a grievance, or even remaining on the committee, would now be "complicated." A couple days later, the dean recommended that I step down from the committee. I knew that I had been cornered, and agreed to step down, going from chair to non-member.

The committee went on to hire the Candidate A. Since assuming her position, the new hire posted a faculty profile page linked from the program's official website. Her faculty profile page betrayed the same awkward prose, poor incorporation of quotes, and other problems of expression typical of first-year student writers, but usually not of professors. The profile also included a glaring grammatical error. I have no idea how she does as a writing professor, other than by what I found on an unofficial ratings site, where the results were not pretty.

My argument here and in general has never been against diversity itself. Quite to the contrary, I have argued that the diversity initiatives undertaken by the program (and no doubt elsewhere) have been mistakenly construed, and hastily and thoughtlessly administered, to the detriment of academic integrity and actual equity. Qualified academics could be found among all population groups. It was incumbent upon the university to find candidates that are qualified, first and foremost, not by their identities per se, but by what they know and are able to do and teach. It is sheer cynicism to suppose that qualified candidates could not be found among minority groups. Resorting to blatant tokenism in hiring and promotion jeopardizes the integrity of higher education and also undermines the objectives that diversity initiatives aim to promote.

Further, when markers of race, gender, gender fluidity, sexual orientation, ethnicity, religion and other factors are the only criteria considered in hiring or admissions, students are cheated, as are those chosen to meet diversity measures on the basis of identity alone. Nothing is more essentialist or constraining than diversity understood strictly in terms of identity. Such a notion of diversity reduces "diverse" people to the status of token bearers of identity markers and relegates them to an impenetrable and largely inescapable identity chrysalis, implicitly eliding their individuality. Meanwhile, there is no necessary connection between identity and ideas, identity and talents, identity and aspirations, or identity and beliefs. Knowing-through-being is in no way limited by identity as such. Epistemological solipsism is a false notion.

Likewise, if we want to foster real diversity in higher education, we had better consider not only diversity of identity but also diversity of thought and perspective. It is this kind of diversity that we are supposed to recognize and foster in the first place.

CHAPTER 10
PRONOUN AS TIPPING POINT

"HIS MAJESTY"

IN THE FALL of 2016, I reached my social justice tipping point. The University of Michigan instituted a policy whereby students were offered a carte blanche pronoun preference opportunity. Students were encouraged to choose existing pronouns or create pronouns of their choice, without limitation. Upon inputting their preferred pronouns into the Wolverine student access portal, they could then demand to be called by these pronouns inside the classroom. No matter what pronouns a student chose, the university promised to honor their choices.

One clever student entered "His Majesty" as his chosen pronoun, and his blasphemous pronoun choice made the news. The satirical trope hilariously underscored the absurdity of gender and pronoun proliferation, and the institutional lunacy that has attempted to keep pace with it. It was a sendup of the university administrators who enacted such a policy but also underscored the absurdity that the social justice movement had managed to have codified within institutions of higher education. I posted a link to an article about the spoof on Facebook, without comment.

I then proceeded to teach for the rest of the afternoon. By the time I noticed the pandemonium, it was too late to manage it. A sustained, billowing, vitriolic, and histrionic reaction had ensued. Hundreds upon hundreds of condemnatory threads and sub-threads multiplied beneath the link. Dozens and dozens of Facebook friends had sent private messages, demanding explanations and retractions. I was accused of betrayal, discursive violence, and transphobia. Many people unfriended and blocked me. I decided "never again." I would no longer accede to the demands of social justice ideologues, or restrain my words, actions, or thoughts according to demands stemming from the social justice creed. That very night I created the Twitter account – the notorious DeplorableNYUProf, with the @antipcnyuprof handle. I began to inveigh against the insidious coercion and control that the social justice creed had imposed on me and many others for far too long.

A MASSIVE SOKAL HOAX

Meanwhile, I am a critic of transgenderism – in particular of the epistemological premises that underwrite it. But criticism of transgender theory no more makes me a transphobe than criticizing Scientology makes one a hater of individual Scientologists.

Transgender theory can be traced to postmodern theoretical ancestors. Again, a radical social and linguistic constructivism is its basis. According to transgender theory, gender – or even, as the story currently goes, "sexual difference" itself – is determined not by chromosomes, anatomy, hormones, or physiology. Such words can only be used ironically or with derision in a Gender Studies or Women's Studies classroom. Instead, gender (or even sex difference) is determined by beliefs about sometimes inconveniently "non-conforming" phenomena, and ultimately, by language, by names. Within transgender theory, empirical sex difference or sex has become insignificant and "problematic" at one and the same time. Sexual characteristics may represent an obstinate yet potentially irrelevant set of features – to be overwritten by a gender identity of choice. Gender identities exist along a spectrum, and, with or without the alteration of secondary sexual characteristics, may metamorphose, sliding between the distant poles of "cis" and trans. According to the office of BGLTQ Student Life at Harvard, gender can "change from day to day," and the institution must recognize a student's gender *du jour*. Gender is thus the new ghost in the machine and the gendered mind occupies and operates an increasingly wrong-sexed body. Transgender theory is a remnant of the philosophical idealism that runs through postmodern theory. It would be inconceivable without its postmodern precursors.

Social justice treats the fields of biology, genetics, evolutionary biology, and evolutionary psychology as anathema, and bars them from its discourse circles using safe spaces and no-platforming. Any reference to these fields has become verboten in social justice milieus. Under social justice ideology, belief claims (TW) trump empirical evidence. Scientific evidence itself is deemed white supremacist, sexist, and patriarchal. While biology is generally rendered mute (or nonconforming) under transgenderism, it may be recuperated and compelled to speak at the behest of transgender theorists and activists, who rely on the so-called "sexed brain" as a safe harbor for an otherwise impermissible biological determinism. Transgender theorists are allowed to assert the utterly essentialist notion of the "female brain" as an explanation for chosen genders. But James Damore, whom Google dispatched from its employment and premises without the slightest consideration of his argument or employment rights, could not argue that sexual difference exists at all. In referring to sex difference as a reality, Damore fell victim to yet another contradiction within leftist social justice identity politics and ideology. Unless transgender activists and ideologues conveniently say otherwise, gender has nothing to do with biology.

Since gender is eminently mutable and potentially decoupled from sex entirely, why would Hormone Replacement Therapy or Gender Reassignment Surgery procedures ever be necessary or advisable? Since, under transgender theory, believing is seeing, why would anyone ever need to change the secondary characteristics of sex? Naturally, the social reception of one's gender may be at stake. But finally, the answer is that secondary sexual characteristics matter if and only if the transgender person says they do. Thus, the meaning of sex and the "reality" of gender hinge on belief. Belief may overwrite inconvenient, "non-conforming" facts, like the "wrong" genitalia. Transitioning is thus sometimes called for; at other times, it's not. Yet without expression, belief is moot. Gender identity requires naming. At the end of the day, gender identity is ultimately determined by language. Thus, the necessity for the linguistic element of social and linguistic constructivism is made manifest.

For another salient example of the proliferation, reach, and dominance of transgender theory beyond the academy, consider the website of Planned Parenthood Federation of America. The agency devotes several pages to gender issues, baldly declaring: "Most kids begin to identify strongly with a gender around age 3. That includes transgender and gender-nonconforming people, who also have a sense of their gender identity at this stage." We are led to believe that three-year-old children not only grasp the complex concept of gender but also gender-nonconforming and transgender three-year-olds know that their own gender identities differ fundamentally from those of gender conformists. Meanwhile, Planned Parenthood is virtually mum about the gender-non-transgressive toddlers, except to admonish new parents to be wary of reinforcing the gender identities and stereotypes that these children represent.

If gender pluralism can be regarded as a religious creed analogous to millennialist Christianity, then "cisgender" persons, or those who accept the genders they were "assigned at birth," are the "left behind" after the Rapture. Such nondescript reprobates toddle into bleak gender-generic futures and continue to reproduce. This state of affairs requires that Planned Parenthood administer rapid transfusions of the current lexicon and parental protocols – before such vulgate-speakers commit child abuse by inducing the trauma of the misgendered child.

Gender is supposedly transparent to young children, yet Planned Parenthood finds it necessary to explain gender and gender identity to adults – the parents and prospective parents of the rising gender-malleable breed. Even as gender-savvy toddlers supposedly recognize their gender identities, their parents and other adults are far from a consensus about gender and gender identities, even in terms of how many gender identities exist. Since the rise of transgender theory in the late 1990s, the female-male sex binary has been buffeted by a tidal wave of proliferating gender identities and pronouns. As new gender identities debut, the ratio of genders to sexes continues to rise. While Oregon and California have implemented a third gender choice on driver's licenses and other forms of identification, in social justice social spaces, genders and their pronouns far outstrip such legislation.

The social and linguistic constructivist claims of social justice ideologues amount to a form of philosophical and social idealism that is enforced with a moral absolutism. Once beliefs are unconstrained by the object world and people can believe anything they like with impunity, the possibility for assuming a pretense of infallibility becomes almost irresistible, especially when the requisite power is available to support such idealism. In fact, given its willy-nilly determination of truth and reality on the basis of beliefs alone, philosophical and social idealism necessarily becomes dogmatic, authoritarian, anti-rational, and effectively religious. Since it sanctions no push-back from the object world and regards it with indifference or disdain, it necessarily encounters push-back from the object world and must double-down. Because it usually contains so much nonsense, the social and philosophical idealism of the social justice creed must be established by force, or the threat of force.

An important example of modern scientific idealism was the adoption of "Lysenkoism" in the Soviet Union. In deference to the "agrobiology" of the Soviet agronomist Trofim Lysenko, from the 1930s to the 1960s, Soviet biology operated under a veritable ban against genetics and its methods. Instead of Mendel's genetics, which are consistent with Darwinism, Lysenko's views of biological heredity were the basis of teaching and research in the Soviet Union. To understand why the Soviets eagerly rejected genetics in favor of Lysenko's hereditary ideas, it's necessary to briefly review the distinction between the Darwinian evolutionary model and that of Jean Baptiste Lamarck, whose *Philosophie Zoologique* (Zoological Philosophy, 1809) laid out his theory of species change. Lysenko was a neo-Lamarckian.

In Lamarckian evolutionary theory, the organism itself strives to modify its habits and ultimately its makeup in response to environmental conditions. Changes in habit result in permanent anatomical and physiological alterations of organisms over time. Such modifications are then passed along to offspring. This process is known as "the inheritance of acquired characteristics." On the other hand, Charles Darwin's mechanism of "natural selection" does not involve the will or the alteration of the individual during its lifetime. It involves the selection of traits by the environment when they serve to increase the differential survivability of an organism's progeny.

The classic example of Lamarck's adaptation theory, often lampooned in contemporary textbooks, concerned the giraffe, whose forelegs and necks, Lamarck suggested, were gradually lengthened as the animal strove to reach the leafy foliage of high-limbed trees, the only source of vegetation available in the arid regions of Africa. In short, under Lamarckian evolutionary theory, the organization of animals always corresponds with their habits, which develop of necessity in connection with their environments. Environments are not fixed or constant, thus organisms must change and develop in conjunction with their changed habitats, eventually leading to the origin of new species.

The environmental determinism of the Lamarckian model fit much better with Soviet socialist ideology. An all-determining environment meant that the composition of society and its members depended on social conditions rather than inherent traits. Likewise, individuals and society could be changed by altering the social environment. The idea that the whole society could be changed by changing the social environment fit well with the socialist objective that sought to mold the world after a socialist image of a *de facto* equality. On the other hand, because inherent characteristics were central to Mendelian genetics and

Darwinian evolution, the Soviets considered the pair to be scientific pillars of capitalist ideology.

In 1928, Lysenko published a paper on "vernalization," or the winterization of crops, which recorded the treatment of wheat seeds with moisture and cold to speed sprouting in the spring. Lysenko claimed that he had achieved a massive increase in crop yields and that the offspring of the vernalized wheat would inherit the acquired characteristics of vernalization bestowed environmentally on the parent crops and thus would flower early. But severe cold and lack of snow destroyed the winter wheat crop. In tandem with Stalin's forced collectivization policies, Lysenkoism resulted in massive crop losses and famines.

Yet in 1948, the Praesidium of the USSR Academy of Science passed a resolution virtually outlawing any biological work that was not based on Lysenko's agrobiology. The Soviet government declared that classical genetics was scientifically inferior to the agrobiology of the Soviet agronomist. Scientists who contradicted Lysenkoism were expected to confess to "errors" and recant or were arrested. Lysenkoism entailed one of the most fearsome witch hunts of modern science – carried out against those who expressed geneticist or Darwinian perspectives.

Lysenkoism is an extraordinary historical example of the attempt to impose social and philosophical idealism on the object world (despite claims that Marxism is philosophically materialist rather than idealist). Minus the gulag and political assassinations for believers in genetics, contemporary transgenderism is reminiscent of Lysenkoism. The transgender movement, with its outright denial of any role for biology in matters of gender and even sexual difference, is no less based on social and philosophical idealism than was Lysenkoism. Transgender theory is contemporary Lysenkoism. And the propagation of transgender theory is akin to a massive Sokal Hoax perpetrated on society at large.

CHAPTER 11
NO ISLAND IS A COMMUNIST

AS I STATED in Chapter Two, as a result of the fallout from my outing as the "'Deplorable' NYU Prof," I found myself besieged and attacked by leftists of all stripes. Likewise, I inevitably questioned my political commitments. Could a political *isolato* such as I had become be a committed communist? The communists that I had known now resembled tyrants more than anything else. I now saw the authoritarianism and embryonic totalitarianism that had been hidden beneath a thin veneer of egalitarian rhetoric. Could I be numbered among a tribe whose members were so monstrous? No, I could not call myself a communist. Besides, to be a communist, one necessarily belonged to a community of some sort. No island is a communist.

I had been ejected from the left and denounced by leftist commentators, including communists. As mentioned above, one commentator suggested that with my supposed defection, I had "pulled a Christopher Hitchens." But I hadn't pulled anything. They had done all the pulling. And pushing. It boggled my mind to think that these leftists, who betrayed such bilious animosity and unrestrained cruelty – some suggesting nothing short of the firing squad – could imagine that their newly made apostate had left them! Who could possibly remain among them? I didn't leave the left. The left left me. Or, rather, the left righted me. By this, I don't mean to suggest that they had turned me into a right-winger. They didn't have that power. I mean that they opened my eyes and allowed me to see rightly. In trying to correct me, they did indeed correct me – but not as they'd hoped. They corrected my vision by forcibly dislodging the scales of their ideology from my eyes.

But could I simply forget twenty-five years of reading, writing, and thinking, and the importance of Marxist and other leftist theory to my intellectual endeavors? I was not a political communist, this was certain. But did that prevent me from using the analytical tools that I had learned from Marxist and other leftist schools and applying them differently? Rather than renouncing such methods, I decided to turn them on the left itself, at least for a while.

One such tool is the Marxist ideological critique, which, inverted, easily applies to socialism itself. For example, Marxists claim that "bourgeois ideology" serves to make the success of the capitalist class appear inevitable and "natural," a result of the superiority of the winners – whereas they see such success as the result of a system within which the workers must always lose due to the structurally-determined demand for profit and exploitation. However, one might similarly argue that socialist ideology serves to mask the failure of the socialist, making his failure appear unnatural, the result of a rigged system. Socialist ideology rationalizes individual failure by laying it at the feet of the system itself, rather than connecting it with its proximate cause, the individual.

Applying the Marxist class analysis, it is important to note that those who advocate socialism are generally not working-class per se. Most are disaffected intellectuals drawn from the petty bourgeoisie. In other words, their political allegiance is rooted in envy and resentment for those who have more power and resources, rather than in the purity of idealism or good will toward the working masses.

But more damning, drawing on the political ideals of socialism itself, the totalitarianism of "actually-existing socialism" can be contrasted with the Marxist claim that socialism represents the only path to "universal human emancipation." Rather than leading to a stateless society of mutual cooperation among free producers, each of whom, as Marx claimed, could "hunt in the morning, fish in the afternoon, rear cattle in the evening, criticize after dinner," socialism has led to the same result every time it's been tried: cultural, economic, political, and social monopoly under a singular state system controlling all areas of life. Rather than allowing a choice of multiple employments, the socialist state becomes the sole employer and determines the worker's exclusive sphere of activity. Rather than withering away as Marx suggested, state power is expanded to enforce cultural, economic, and social monopoly. Rather than politics disappearing as alleged, an official socialist-communist party monopolizes state power so that the system is unchallenged in other spheres. Instead of disappearing, the state remains necessary for enforcing socialist monopolies and it uses all the means necessary to do so, including terror. Terror is not optional, but rather, as even Marx himself admitted, inevitable. And, far from being limited to Stalin's reign, the terror began under Lenin soon after the revolution and continued with every subsequent communist leader, including Stalin, Mao, Pol Pot, and Castro.

My rejection of Marxism began with this political critique of totalitarianism. But my rationale soon widened to include a recognition of its guaranteed economic failure. Well before the collapse of the Soviet bloc, Ludwig von Mises showed that far from representing the only rational economic system that could remedy the "anarchy" of the market, the socialist planned economy is utterly irrational. Its irrationality is due to the elimination of the essential indices for determining rational production and distribution – namely, prices. Von Mises showed that prices represent the incredibly thick and vital data sets required for allocating productive resources for commodity production and calibrating these to demand. Socialism is irrational because by beginning without prices for the machinery of production, no rational criteria could ever emerge for allocating resources to specific production processes. And when unpriced consumer goods are added to the mix, the chaos multiplies – unless, that is, political force is applied, and it always is. Eliminating prices, the socialist economy cannot provide the feedback loops required for determining what to produce or how much of it to produce. Cancerous, over-sized productive capacities in one sector of the economy are paralleled by relatively anemic productive capacities in another, and so on. And resorting to the labor theory of value won't fix the problem. The socially average amount of labor time required to produce a commodity, even if it determines a commodity's value (a doubtful claim in any case), is by no means an adequate index for determining the amount of resources to devote to its production.

This means that socialism fails not only at resource allocation but also at the economic representation of the people it claims to champion. Absent price mechanisms, economic "voters," or consumers, have no way to voice their needs and wants. Production and distribution must be based on the non-democratic decision-making of centralized authorities. Those who really care about the working masses must reject socialism for its incapacity to establish economic democracy, its most fundamental reason for being.

As such, my renunciation of Marxism has not been a mere matter of rejecting social justice ideology and then extrapolating backwards historically. Using the terms "cultural Marxism" and "neo-Marxism" in terchangeably to refer to social justice and postmodernism is mistaken. First, as I showed in Chapter 5, the term "cultural Marxism" refers to a particular Marxist theory and strategy inaugurated by Antonio Gramsci – working to establish "cultural hegemony" in order to effect socialist revolution.

Second, the substitution of special identity groups advocated for by social justice activists for the working class championed by Marxists does not lead to an identical or nearly identical politics. With the working class as a lever, Marxism proposes to overcome its nemesis – the capitalist class, which maintains the class system, including a class-based system of production and resource allocation. Social justice, on the other hand, aims at little more than debunking particular identity groups from atop a putative social hierarchy, knocking them from their supposed positions of totemic privilege, and replacing them with members of supposedly subordinated groups.

Third, in Chapter 5, I told why Marxism and postmodernism can't be equated. I'll restate it here. While postmodern theory is anti-capitalist, it not only rejects capitalism but also other "totalizing" systems, or "meta-narratives," including even the major system proposed to counter capitalism – Marxism itself.

Nevertheless, a lineage can be established between these three relatives. Postmodern theory may be properly understood as the "missing link" between the older Marxist left and the contemporary social justice left. Yet many mutations have occurred within leftist political ideology in the evolution from Marxism to social justice. In order to understand the contemporary social justice left, then, I have examined postmodern theory in some depth. To understand the specific *political effects* of social justice ideology, including its effects on the older left, which it has all but completely engulfed, it is necessary to understand social justice as "practical postmodernism," or the politics of postmodern theory.

CHAPTER 12
THE POLITICS OF POSTMODERN THEORY

W HEN IN RECENT YEARS I noticed the surfacing of the social justice creed and movement – first on the Internet and later in the university – I instantly recognized its genetic makeup from having studied its parentage in postmodern theory. Although the ideas that had been sheltered under the broad umbrella of postmodern theory had lost much of their currency where they once thrived – in the humanities and especially English departments of colleges and universities – elsewhere, in other, perhaps more important areas, they garnered more currency than ever before. While postmodern theory itself had virtually died, like most parents, it was survived by children. As the children of postmodern theory became adult-sized, they occupied newly transformed minds, bodies, and identities and began to populate the world. These children of postmodern theory became known as the social justice warriors.

Given its roots in postmodern theory, as I stated in the Preface, I came to think of social justice ideology as "practical postmodernism," or "applied postmodern theory." Social justice warriors are "practical postmodernists," although they don't know it.

With the rise of social justice by the second term of the Obama administration, a transmutation in the polis began. The transmutation involved the personalization of the political. Rather than undertaking mass action, for example, the social justice approach involves calling out individuals for their supposed failures as political beings. Rather than attacking capitalism (as in socialism) or dismantling the patriarchy (as in radical feminism), the social justice movement acts as if political change can only be brought about by taking down one politically evil person at a time. The social justice movement individualizes its targets. It has gained momentum by hyper-personalizing the political, or, as the leftist critics of "neoliberalism" might say, by privatizing politics. This can be seen clearly in its most recent incarnation – the #MeToo movement.

But the old New Left slogan – "the personal is political" – does not adequately capture the change in politics represented by social justice ideology. The New Left's mantra meant that individual behaviors matter but also that they reflect broader political and social trends, while contributing to them. As a New Leftist might have put it, being a jerk to one's wife is not only wrong in itself but also points to the strong possibility that one discriminates against women more broadly, and thus contributes to a generalized misogyny. Whatever one might think about its goals or actual outcomes, in New Left politics, individual change was believed to be both local and universal; the New Left sought personal and broader political change at one and the same time.

With social justice, on the other hand, politics is restricted to and distorted by the personal, while the personal is effectively effaced and replaced by politics. The personal is not political; it does not flow into and become part of a political movement. Instead, the political is made narrowly personal, while the personal becomes nothing but politics. The individual person is reduced to a mere emblem of political meaning, while politics is reduced to the political (moral) worthiness, or lack thereof, of individual persons. Politics becomes individual morality based on social justice standards.

According to Derrida, co-founder of deconstruction, language is a signifying system with no necessary connection to anything beyond itself. Deconstruction suggested that the ontological entities to which language supposedly refers reside only within language. "There is no outside of text." Social justice activism is deconstruction "in action." As in deconstruction, in social justice activism, there is no outside of the text. Politics is reduced by social justice warriors to a series of semaphores – Facebook statuses, tweets, kneel-downs during the singing of the U.S. national anthem, and so forth – gestures that merely signify themselves and therefore effectively signify nothing at all. While personal expression and behavior are assiduously policed by social justice activists, the political is reduced to a semiotic field for the identification, location, and condemnation of individuals within a political and moral matrix.

Social justice activism is limited to particular forms of textual signaling, primarily to "virtue signaling" and "call-out." Virtue signaling is the announcement of one's political (and moral) worthiness and virtue, often by means of an implicit or explicit comparison of oneself to politically "evil" others. Callout refers to the ritualized, direct denunciations of politically evil individuals and groups. It sometimes calls for their loss of employment in addition to their loss of social standing. In "Blame the Left for the Rise of Moralizing in America," *Federalist* commentator John Daniel Davidson gives examples of social justice virtue signaling and call out – *The New Yorker*'s histrionics over Chick-fil-A's "infiltration" of New York City, gun-control activist David Hogg's calls for boycotts of Fox News host Laura Ingraham, and the protestor with a megaphone shouting in Starbucks at a clerk's face over the case of supposed racial discrimination at a Philadelphia location. In these and myriad other incidents, social justice activism amounts to mere accusations and denunciations but includes little or no action and certainly involves no good works.

The premium that social justice places on virtue signaling and call out has been especially conspicuous in condemnations of the world's biggest pop star, Taylor Swift. For the crime of remaining politically taciturn, Swift has faced charges of "fake feminism," "white feminism," "spineless feminism," and worse. When droves jumped on the Twitter hash tag bandwagon to condemn the so-called "Muslim ban," Swift instead posted links to a video she made with a Muslim artist and was widely denounced. When Kesha Rose Sebert tried to end her recording contract with the producer she claimed had drugged and raped her a decade earlier, Swift was called out and condemned for failing to tweet in support. Withholding such tweets was deemed unforgivable, despite or even because Swift donated $250,000 to the artist and her family instead. Recording artist Demi Lovato aimed a blistering subtweet at Swift: "Take something to Capitol Hill [to the Women's March] or actually speak out about something and then I'll be impressed." As if impressing Lovato and others like her is the objective, and as if marching in a pussy hat or "speaking out" (virtue signaling) tops philanthropy.

In the end, under social justice ideology, the political is reduced to a textual system without "real" referents or actions upon those referents, a symbolic register of virtue signaling or refusing to virtue signal. To signal or not to signal – that is the question.

CONCLUSION:
LOOKING FORWARD

RE-SECULARIZING THE UNIVERSITY

I HAD PLANNED to conclude by speculating on the reasons that social justice has been adopted so extensively – not only in education but also in information technology, mass media, the "deep state," and other corporate and state milieus. Evidence of social justice adherence in dominant digital media firms is extensive and includes censorship by YouTube, James Damore's Google gender imbroglio, Twitter's blatant anti-conservative bias, and Facebook's left-leaning content mining of user data and manipulation of journalistic and advertising content. As for the deep state – the CIA, FBI, and other intelligence agencies – social justice has also breached the walls of their covert hideaways.

The question is, how and why? Although I have decided not to yield much space to this line of thinking, I will suggest that these and other institutions clearly find the ideology useful. While initially succumbing to social justice trends, organizations came to recognize that the ideology provides subsidiary benefits, including but not limited to the allegiance of new identity constituencies and the disciplining of other subjects, especially members of hitherto "privileged" groups. But it is unlikely that extended speculation could ever be definitive or ultimately satisfying. So, I've decided to turn to a proposed solution instead.

I've given many reasons to reject social justice ideology. But "negative" efforts must be accompanied by "positive" recommendations. Here I will focus on the recognition that the social justice doctrine is an undeclared but routinely observed and enforced state-corporate religion. Likewise, a replacement ethos must be offered, one that neither infringes individual rights nor contravenes other cherished belief systems, whether religious or secular.

Having pointed to the many ways that social justice stymies academic freedom, freedom of inquiry, freedom of religion, and even freedom of conscience, the next step is to pin the religious label on it. Social justice is religious partly because it justifies itself not on evidence or rationality but on the basis of belief and ritual. This is not a condemnation of religion but merely a characterization of social justice as religious. The problem is that in the university and elsewhere, these beliefs have passed for knowledge and as impartial policy. Social justice has attained sacrosanct status by promoting its beliefs and rituals as unassailable. Recognizing that our institutions of education have adopted a religious creed should go a long way in removing social justice from its parapet and installing a new, higher-order creed in its place. I will call this new higher-order creed "post-secularism."

The principle I recommend is parallel to that adopted by the founders of the United States of America. The founders believed in and established religious freedom on the basis of a non-religious (although not an anti-religious) state. North American education must be rebuilt and reinvigorated along these lines – by introducing and reestablishing a truly inclusive, non-partisan, non-religious, non-sectarian, and supervisory "post-secularism." Post-secularism is a term that recently has been introduced by theorists to underscore the persistence of religious beliefs, while privileging neither the religious or non-religious, and to acknowledge the hitherto biased and non-neutral character of a supposedly unbiased and neutral secularism. Post-secularism is a perspective that recognizes the old secularism's anti-religious bias and that oversees and mitigates inter-religious and religious and secular conflict. In the post-secular university, religious and secular creeds will be recognized and included under a common umbrella.

Given that social justice is one religious creed among many, it follows that the remaking of the university cannot involve an attempt to utterly eradicate the social justice creed or to drive its believers to the margins – where, falsely, they believe they already reside. Successful reformation must allow social justice ideology to remain in existence while it is removed from its current position as policy-maker, arbiter of expression and inquiry, and censor. Only by relegating social justice to the position of one among many other belief systems can the university successfully absorb the creed without remaining hostage to it. But we can no longer allow social justice to serve as the basis for university policies, politics, or pedagogy. Social justice must be subordinated to a higher-level, post-secular ethos, as merely one among many belief options.

AND THE TWEET GOES ON

While I have endured the shunning of the vast majority of my immediate colleagues at NYU, the ejection from political groups, and the damnation of the left, I have received support from a few other academics, including Gad Saad, Jordan Peterson, and Bret Weinstein. I am working with like-minded people to establish a counter to safe spaces, a consortium for challenging echo chambers and promoting exchange spaces to build consensus on fundamental, post-secular, reason-based principles. I have also turned to the advice of those working toward similar goals and developing cognate structures. One such associate is the NYU social psychologist and founder of Heterodox Academy, Jonathan Haidt.

Although I considered social justice to be a religious doctrine before we met in the spring of 2017, Haidt validated my view. He suggested that we find ourselves in the midst of a new moral order that has emerged on almost all college and university campuses and is vying for members and supporters. The old discursive and behavioral rules no longer apply. He characterized this package of moral imperatives as equivalent, psychologically, to religious fundamentalism and suggested that its believers are passionately committed to their beliefs. Therefore, he argued, nothing I might say or write could change their minds. For those who belong to this new moral order, he continued, I am the equivalent of a devil. I had mistaken my interview in the student newspaper and subsequent commentary with acceptable criticism of institutions, yet my detractors regarded it as sacrilege.

It was after this meeting that I hearkened back to my studies of nineteenth-century British Secularism, recalling the legal persecution and social opprobrium that the early Secularists endured at the hands of bigots, cowardly conformists, and state apparatuses. I have experienced nothing remotely comparable, though there is a clear analogy. In early twenty-first-century academia, replete with its attendant religious dogma, I am a new kind of secularist recommending a new kind of secularism.

Yet there is a wrinkle in this comparison, one that recapitulates the decisive split in the nineteenth-century Secularist movement. In my opposition to social justice, I have arguably vacillated between positions that reflect the two major Secularist approaches: the "positive" camp of Secularism's founder and coiner of the word, George Jacob Holyoake, and the staunchly oppositional "negative" camp headed by Secularism's bombastic, anti-clerical, Bible-bashing subsequent leader, Charles Bradlaugh. Far from advocating the destruction of religion, Holyoake founded Secularism as an alternative to atheism. He imagined and fostered the cooperation of secular and religious members operating under a common umbrella. For Holyoake, the secular and religious were to be understood as complementary and co-constituting aspects of what he called Secularism. Bradlaugh, on the other hand, argued that Secularism was atheist and had to destroy religious belief.

Haidt suggested that I moderate my tone and use less incendiary and more academic, "inclusive," and conditional language – which would resemble something like the contemporary equivalent of Holyoake's approach. I had celebrated Holyoake's brand of Secularism in my book, *Nineteenth-Century British Secularism*, and elsewhere. Yet, amidst this twenty-first-century academic religiosity, I had been cast by opponents and even some allies in the position of a Bradlaugh. Which posture would I adopt, or did I no longer have a choice?

My answer has been "both." So, while in this book I have used more measured and scholarly writing on the topic, my readers should not expect my Twitter or Facebook pronouncements to become less strident any time soon.

ACKNOWLEDGMENTS

I N THE CASE of this book, I must recognize not only those who helped me with the text itself but also those who supported me, in one way or another, through one of the most difficult periods if not the most difficult period of my adult life. In some cases, they are the same people. These include a few academics but mostly friends from outside academia, those without the prejudices of my colleagues or the animus of the "regressive left."

In terms of the writing, I am indebted to the following persons, who read various versions of text and whom I'll list in alphabetical order for no other reason than that listing them in order of importance would be almost impossible: Adam Bellow, Diana Hume George, Maggi Laureys, Mark Crispin Miller, Paul Musgrave, Lori Price, John Tangney, and Martha Woodmansee. I would like to thank Julian Vigo for her feedback on gender-critical feminism. I am indebted to Kendra Mallock for connecting me with the New English Review Press. I would like to thank Rebecca Bynum for agreeing to publish this controversial book.

In addition to reading the text, Diana Hume George, Mark Crispin Miller, John Tangney, and Martha Woodmansee were among the few academic friends who also lent emotional and intellectual support. Additionally, many friends on Facebook and Twitter have been indispensable for their continuous encouragement. I cannot name you all but you know who you are. I thank my attorneys, whom I hope do not mind being numbered among my friends: Brett Joshpe and Ed Paltzik. I am grateful to Mike Keenan for his expertise in media and photography and his support of my media campaign. I thank Matthew Tyrmand for lending his media-savvy expertise and guidance, as well as his immense political knowledge. I owe a special thanks to Lori Price, who provided me a soft-landing site when I fell out with my university and life partner at the same time, and whose encouragement has been unwavering.

I especially want to thank my children: John-Michael, Molly, and Dylan – for putting up with and helping me during this tumultuous time and for lending their support in various ways: in long conversations about the topic with John-Michael and especially Dylan, and in conversations with Molly, who helped me check my motives and psychology with reference to my professional situation.

Parts of the Preface and Chapter 10 were published previously as "'Social Justice' and Its Postmodern Parentage" in *Academic Questions*. 31.2. (10 April 2018): 1-10.

Appendix A:
Best Tweets

Michael Rectenwald @antipcnyuprof May 2
Cultural appropriation is an utterly inane notion. No one *owns*
culture. Thus, no one can appropriate it. And all cultures are hybrids.
Cultural purity is a myth. Therefore, ending "cultural appropriation"
would mean worldwide cultural disintegration.

Michael Rectenwald @antipcnyuprof Apr 29
The left believes in sacrificing individuals for the good of the collective
-- even if they have to kill all the individuals to do so.

Michael Rectenwald @antipcnyuprof Apr 8
Some leftist has just told me that I've fallen far intellectually since
leaving the left and that I have also lost academic status. In his estimation, I'm sure I have fallen. But his estimation does not matter. Mine
does. And, he happens to be empirically wrong. No surprise.

Michael Rectenwald @antipcnyuprof Apr 7
I wish the Democrats would stop using insolent children as human
shields [in the March for Our Lives Movement].

Michael Rectenwald @antipcnyuprof · Mar 28
A commitment to empirical science and technical thinking is now verboten for engineers. What's next? A commitment to reality privileges sanity at the expense of schizophrenic otherkins.

Profs warn that 'commitment to empirical science' hurts women
Four professors warn that the "hegemony of meritocratic ideology" and "masculine culture" in engineering courses are oppressive to female stu...
campusreform.org

♡ 6   ⟲ 11   ♡ 31   ᴵᶦᶦ

Michael Rectenwald @antipcnyuprof Mar 25
In other news, yesterday, "protesters" joined forces with the deep state to clamor for the curtailment of their rights.

Michael Rectenwald @antipcnyuprof Mar 25
This new "protest movement" [March for Our Lives] is a simulacrum. In a very real sense, it's not real.

Michael Rectenwald @antipcnyuprof Mar 24
Blue checkmarks are for blue-pilled denizens of the matrix.

Michael Rectenwald @antipcnyuprof Mar 17
Close your eyes & imagine a world full of self-replicating little Stalins. Now open your eyes. You live in that world. It's called "social justice" & the little Stalins are SJWs. SJW = Stalin, Just Weirder.

Michael Rectenwald @antipcnyuprof · Mar 16

Classical liberalism involves *values* pluralism but not postmodern epistemological subjectivism and relativism.

Michael Rectenwald

57 mins · 🌐 ▾

"A pluralistic society necessarily has many different goals and many different definitions of what is good and just. There may be justifications for granting special privileges to the underprivileged, but the assertion of a monopolistic ethic in a pluralistic society tends to result simply in the expression of competing ethical ends through hypocrisy and subterfuge.

"The most troubling assumption in both the perspective and the theory of social justice involves power. If justice is a matter of organizing society in the best interests of the least advantaged, then the quest for justice necessitates unending efforts to reorganize society in the name of those interests. A society, however, is not a specific institutional entity or even a set of procedures, like a legal system. A society is the total sum of interactions and historically shaped patterns of interactions among people. The goal of reorganizing society as a whole, then, is essentially a goal of reshaping how people choose to live and think. This goal is implicitly totalitarian, although it certainly does not necessarily lead to totalitarianism because of the many real-world barriers to translating moral goals into political action."

-- Carl L. Bankston III, "Social Justice Cultural Origins of a Perspective and a Theory."

"Classical liberals do not present themselves as marketing any particular view of

human excellence. Rather they defend institutions that allow individuals to make their own choices about how to live."

💬 1   🔁 2   ♡ 21   ⷾ

Michael Rectenwald @antipcnyuprof Mar 16

Postmodernism is usually anti-modern and "social justice" is just a postmodern (figural) form of tribal blood-letting.

Michael Rectenwald @antipcnyuprof Mar 16

Promote liberty over enforced values, esp. when those values abrogate liberty & otherwise have little to recommend them other than force itself.

Michael Rectenwald @antipcnyuprof Mar 16
I now use Marxist analytical methods to criticize Marxists. For example, Marxists claim that "bourgeois ideology" serves to make the success of the capitalist seem "natural." I argue that similarly, socialist ideology serves to make the failure of the socialist seem unnatural.

Michael Rectenwald @antipcnyuprof Mar 15
Given a choice, people will generally prefer chaos to the ordered chains of tyranny.

Michael Rectenwald @antipcnyuprof Mar 11
The safe space expands to the size of the universe: Student paper apologizes for printing photo of conservative scholar http://www.legitgov.org/Student-paper-apologizes-printing-photo-conservative-scholar via @legitgov

Michael Rectenwald @antipcnyuprof Mar 10
I walked into a hipster coffee shop and asked for a cup of 'gender fluid.' The cashier just pointed to the barista.

Michael Rectenwald @antipcnyuprof Mar 10
If I thought that the carriers of "social justice" ideology could be reached, I would work to do so. I don't so I try to advise those who have not yet been infected to avoid this ideology like the plague. My advice to the uninfected: read Nietzsche for an inoculation.

Michael Rectenwald @antipcnyuprof Mar 10
"Social justice" ideology is an insidious social virus.

Michael Rectenwald @antipcnyuprof · Mar 8
Congratulations! So, is it fair to say that you're not oppressed if indeed you are "dominating?"

> **Jemima McEvoy** @jemimanews
> Women weren't allowed to enroll in college until little over a century ago, now we're fucking dominating. Happy International Women's Day — your gender means nothing but power // thanks to all the women who allowed us to get to this point
> Show this thread

♡ 7   ↻ 4   ♡ 44

Michael Rectenwald @antipcnyuprof Mar 8
It is not enough to merely dismiss postmodernism (postmodern theories). Postmodernism must be explained, analyzed, and demonstrated to be mistaken. Then, one must locate its manifestations in the culture and show how Pomo has produced them. Finally, one works to extirpate it.

Michael Rectenwald @antipcnyuprof Mar 7
Hey poll parrot and robotic chanting leftists: you're losing the actual war of the intellect. Your minds are so utterly flabby from disuse that it's almost unfair to ask you to express a thought.

Michael Rectenwald @antipcnyuprof Mar 7
Social justice advice: "Hurry up and call someone a racist, lest you be called one!"

Michael Rectenwald @antipcnyuprof Mar 6
Diversity is a code word for uniformity of thought.

Michael Rectenwald @antipcnyuprof Feb 28
Socialism is not a plan to overcome the ruling class and establish the collective ownership of the means of production. It is a plan to *consolidate* the ownership of the means of production in the hands of the oligarchy, with the masses as "equal."

Michael Rectenwald @antipcnyuprof Feb 28
The leftist denial of the mass murders of communist regimes is comparable to Holocaust denialism. If western leftists think they have it worse than the average Soviet citizen, they are either insane, historically illiterate, under a thick ideological shroud, or all of the above.

Michael Rectenwald @antipcnyuprof Feb 28
Romantic utopianism is the opiate of the leftists.

Michael Rectenwald @antipcnyuprof · Feb 26
That the Bolsheviks mass-murdered workers in the name of th workers'
revolution is one of the most sinister ironies of modern history.

> **Michael Rectenwald** @antipcnyuprof
> If leftists think that capitalists have been violent against striking workers,
> they ought to read about how the Bolsheviks treated them -- sending them
> to concentration camps, or, with bullets to their heads, to their graves,
> usually a ditch in the ground. drive.google.com/file/d/14EBiF1...

♡ 1   ⇄ 13   ♡ 36

Michael Rectenwald @antipcnyuprof Feb 25
I'm trans-planetary. Mars is Venus, Venus is Mars. To hell with ontology!
Empirical reality must take a backseat to my beliefs!

Michael Rectenwald @antipcnyuprof Feb 25
The moon is the sun because I say it is. And if you disagree you're a
bigot.

Michael Rectenwald @antipcnyuprof Feb 23
Trudeau is emblematic of Western cultural pandering & an endless
apology ethos.

Michael Rectenwald @antipcnyuprof Feb 21
Political correctness is a code to silence dissent as western society
is razed. The culture wars will erupt into violence, pitting those who
defend western values vs. leftists, their "allies," & the rulers who want
to consign western civilization to oblivion.

Michael Rectenwald @antipcnyuprof Feb 19
.@TuckerCarlson points to the real authoritarian threat today and
it's not coming from Trump. It's coming from the very people who call
Trump authoritarian. The left is the authoritarian threat today.

Michael Rectenwald @antipcnyuprof Feb 12
A shameless will to power will be the inevitable response to all of the
shackling and shaming of "privilege."

Michael Rectenwald @antipcnyuprof Feb 7
Watching @IngrahamAngle I see the right doesn't know a fraction
re: the insanity of the identitarian left. No father-daughter dances?
Try people who identify as "yellow-scaled wingless dragonkin" & "an
expansive ornate building!" It's WAY crazier than you think! Ask @
JamesADamore

Michael Rectenwald @antipcnyuprof Feb 4
Under the rhetorical veneer of egalitarianism spouted by the left,
totalitarian impulses and utterly insane irrationality lurk.

Michael Rectenwald @antipcnyuprof Feb 3
The "Russian collusion" narrative is an empty, evidence-free smoke-
screen, a deflection invented to protect and promote Hillary Clinton
and to destroy Trump in case he won. The "resistance" is rooting for
the deep state and their oligarchical overlords.

 Michael Rectenwald @antipcnyuprof · Feb 3
The infiltration of social justice ideology in K-12. What will these programs be
sending to universities if not robotic social justice zealots unable to think or
evaluate other perspectives without hostility? weeklystandard.com/inside-a-
publi...!

Inside a Public School Social Justice Factory
For decades, the public schools of Edina, Minnesota, were the gold
standard among the state's school districts. Edina is an upscale suburb of...
weeklystandard.com

○ 7   ⟲ 15   ♡ 34

Michael Rectenwald @antipcnyuprof Feb 1
Outrage mongers are like the robotic squids in The Matrix. They are mindless, merciless, robotic replicants. Imagining they are virtuous, they represent vile hatred. Imagining they are radical, they are disciplinary tools of the statist, punitive, dehumanizing matrix.

Michael Rectenwald @antipcnyuprof Jan 31
"Social justice" ideologues both inside and outside of academia do not make arguments or have what we can call "thoughts." They merely piece together vacuous plug-n-play social justice phrases like children playing w/blocks -- only they're less creative than children.

Michael Rectenwald @antipcnyuprof Jan 31
You'd think that FBI and other intelligence agents would know better than to call a secret society "the secret society."

Michael Rectenwald @antipcnyuprof Jan 30
As diversity extends its reign, everything becomes the same.

⇅ Michael Rectenwald Retweeted

Fox News ✔ @FoxNews · Jan 29
"[The Diversity, Equity and Inclusion group] said I was guilty for the structure of my thinking. So, basically I had the wrong kinds of thoughts." — @antipcnyupro @nyuniversity professor known for tweets that fight back against PC culture
fxn.ws/2mvIDZd

► MICHAEL RECTENWALD | PROFESSOR SUING NYU
'DEPLORABLE' PROFESSOR SUES NYU

◯ 77   ⭢ 266   ♡ 598

Michael Rectenwald @antipcnyuprof Jan 27
I'm looking forward to getting more money in my paycheck thanks to the tax cut. Must be fascism.

Michael Rectenwald @antipcnyuprof Jan 26
The first social function to be completely replaced by robots will be leftist activism. Repetitive sloganeering is something robots can do quite well.

 Michael Rectenwald @antipcnyuprof · Jan 26 ⌄
Hint: fascism was collectivist, anti-individualist, philosophically idealist and held to social constructivism. What contemporary political contingent does most sound like?

Michael Rectenwald @antipcnyuprof
I bet there's not one #Antifa member who could tell you who founded fascism or what its actual core premises and assertions were.

♡ 9   ↻ 43   ♡ 88

Michael Rectenwald @antipcnyuprof Jan 24
I deplore all forms of totalitarianism. But Left totalitarianism has killed many more millions than any other kind.

Michael Rectenwald @antipcnyuprof · Jan 16

"For simpletons, there is no difference between hurt feelings and defamation. The social justice left is not only a mob, it is a mob without a single individual that can understand the meaning of words, and the difference between damaging someone's actual career and stating an opinion that bothers someone. It's not MY feelings that matter here. The stupidity of social justice leftists is beyond confounding."

◯ 77   ⟲ 34   ♡ 90

Michael Rectenwald @antipcnyuprof Jan 3
Why wouldn't a white guy calling for white genocide begin with himself?

Michael Rectenwald @antipcnyuprof Jan 2
When the westerner's cultural objects are adopted by the "subordinate" culture, it's called "cultural imperialism." When the westerner adopts the cultural artifacts of the subordinate, it's "cultural appropriation." Basically whitey can't win bc whitey has supposedly already won.

Michael Rectenwald @antipcnyuprof Jan 1
"Years" are a social construction created by the cisheterornormative white capitalist patriarchy. There is no actual time. But Happy New Year.

Michael Rectenwald @antipcnyuprof 13 Dec 2017
Communism is the bastard child of capitalism, a leaching, vampiric attempt to reap the rewards of capitalism to satisfy the ressentiment of a few petty bourgeois intellectuals.

Michael Rectenwald @antipcnyuprof · 28 Nov 2017
.@KeithObermann, Your work is done because you are washed-up and insane. You're utterly unhinged and should be investigated for your serial threats against Trump & Co. Seek psychiatric care. If Twitter weren't a biased "social justice" sewer hole, you'd have been banned long ago.

Keith Olbermann @KeithOlbermann
The last tweet ABOUT the last edition of #TheResistanceGQ. My work here is done. As a matter of fact, so is Trump's

THE E
9:52

10 18 61

Michael Rectenwald @antipcnyuprof 9 Nov 2017
The social justice ideologues are the contemporary equivalents of the Pharisees. Jesus hated Phariseeism because by ostentatiously praying in public the Pharisees virtue-signaled to the crowd even as they sinned against (abused, harassed, defamed and libeled) their neighbors.

Michael Rectenwald @antipcnyuprof 23 Oct 2017
I haven't mentioned this bizarre fact: NYU put my office in the Russian department.

Michael Rectenwald @antipcnyuprof 11 Oct 2017
Campus "radicals" are the most pusillanimous, conformist, anti-individual & predictable ppl on earth. Not a singular individual among them.

Michael Rectenwald @antipcnyuprof 17 Sep 2017
How many in Antifa may be simply sociopaths hiding under a banner of virtue to commit violence?

Michael Rectenwald @antipcnyuprof · 7 Sep 2017
The best real-life depiction of PC/social justice authoritarianism imaginable.
"Diversity" -- at the end of a gun.

◯ 3   ⇄ 14   ♡ 42

Michael Rectenwald @antipcnyuprof 3 Sep 2017
Poor whites earn liberals 0 virtue points-except as butt of jokes,
when called racists or laughed at on rare, distasteful trips to Wal-
Mart.

Michael Rectenwald @antipcnyuprof 29 Aug 2017
"Resistance?" Resist the narrow-banding & force-feeding of a consis-
tently homogeneous ideological pap by a monopoly of mass & social
media.

Michael Rectenwald @antipcnyuprof · 29 Aug 2017 ⌄
SJW AI agents construct syntagms from pre-fabricated units of phrasing found on the web. SJW do not have what we call "thoughts."

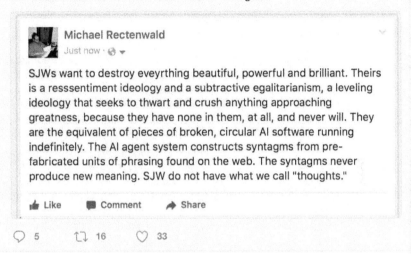

Michael Rectenwald
Just now · 🌐 ⯆

SJWs want to destroy eveyrthing beautiful, powerful and brilliant. Theirs is a resssentiment ideology and a subtractive egalitarianism, a leveling ideology that seeks to thwart and crush anything approaching greatness, because they have none in them, at all, and never will. They are the equivalent of pieces of broken, circular AI software running indefinitely. The AI agent system constructs syntagms from pre-fabricated units of phrasing found on the web. The syntagms never produce new meaning. SJW do not have what we call "thoughts."

👍 Like   💬 Comment   ➔ Share

🗨 5   ⇄ 16   ♡ 33

Michael Rectenwald @antipcnyuprof 28 Aug 2017
Every SJW --no matter which of 72 genders it claims to be -- is agent Smith at the core.

Michael Rectenwald @antipcnyuprof 28 Aug 2017
Agent Smith works at Google, YouTube, Facebook & Twitter & hunts red-pilled escapees to permanently delete them.

Michael Rectenwald @antipcnyuprof 28 Aug 2017
Agent Smith is an SJW multiplying by the thousands and killing every red-pilled person he can find.

Michael Rectenwald @antipcnyuprof · 25 Aug 2017
Friedrich Nietzsche, On the Genealogy of Morals. What contemporaries do thes
people he refers to sound like to you?

Michael Rectenwald
Just now · 🌐 ▾

"And how clever such an ambition makes people! For let's admire the
skillful counterfeiting with which people here imitate the trademarks of
virtue, even its resounding tinkle, the golden sound of virtue. They've
now taken a lease on 'virtue' entirely for themselves, these weak and
hopeless invalids—there's no doubt about that. 'We alone are the good
men, the just men'—that's how they speak: 'We alone are the homines
bonae voluntatis [men of good will].' They wander around among us like
personifications of reproach, like warnings to us, as if health, success,
strength, pride, and a feeling of power were inherently depraved things,
for which people must atone someday, atone bitterly. How they thirst to
be hangmen! Among them there are plenty of people disguised as judges
seeking revenge. They always have the word '[Social] Justice' in their
mouths, like poisonous saliva, with their mouths always pursed,
constantly ready to spit at anything which does not look discontented
and goes on its way in good spirits."

Friedrich Nietzsche, On the Genealogy of Morals. What contemporaries
do these people he refers to sound like to you?

  💬 6   🔁 44   ♡ 97

Michael Rectenwald @antipcnyuprof 22 May 2017
The first step in SJW indoctrination is to preclude independent
thought by providing the new indoctrinee w/pre-fab phrases for regular use.

Michael Rectenwald @antipcnyuprof 22 May 2017
A whole lot of SJW zombies on me now, hurling their 5-yr-old plays
on my last name & regurgitated phraseology from the SJW language
store.

Michael Rectenwald @antipcnyuprof 22 May 2017
Notice the SJW idea that "some language is violence" matters only
when it affects them. They hurl any invectives they wish and it's fine.

Michael Rectenwald @antipcnyuprof 22 May 2017
Judith Butler said gender was a performance. But it's *gender studies* that is the performance, and bad acting at that.

Michael Rectenwald @antipcnyuprof 21 May 2017
Twitter's not social media, it's *social justice media*-it's for "inclusion," a code word for *exclusion* of all but PC authoritarian views.

Michael Rectenwald @antipcnyuprof 20 May 2017
Much of what pass[es] for scholarship in the humanities & social sciences amounts to highly formalized virtue-signaling rituals.

Michael Rectenwald @antipcnyuprof 19 May 2017
Why can't liberals (illiberals) & illiberal leftists see that their ideology ("social justice," etc.) is actually serving ruling interests?

 Michael Rectenwald @antipcnyuprof · 17 May 2017
Genders galore! Whatever you say! But make me declare that sexual difference does not exist in human beings? To that I will not accede.

 Michael Rectenwald
Just now · 🔒 ▾

I don't care what gender(s) or non-gender(s) people claim for themselves. That is entirely their prerogative and I have no objection to anyone's gender identification, whatever it may or may not be. I will accede to their self-identification, including a relatively reasonable pronoun semantics.

But don't try to make me subscribe and declare true that sexual difference does not exist in human beings. This claim is sheerly a matter of anti-empirical religiosity, and I will not pretend that it's true. Take me to the gulag if it comes down to that. But sexual difference does exist in human beings and without sexual difference human beings could not reproduce -- unless, that is, we turned into asexual organisms, which is a great unlikelihood.

👍 Like   💬 Comment   ➤ Share

💬 5   ↻ 5   ♡ 22   ⅲ

Michael Rectenwald @antipcnyuprof 16 May 2017
The shaming techniques that the Left engages in--callout culture, self-criticism, privilege checking--all have Maoism as their provenance.

Michael Rectenwald @antipcnyuprof 15 May 2017
We are now dealing with a lunatic cult of vast proportions. It's like Heaven's Gate, only without the Nikes.

Michael Rectenwald @antipcnyuprof 15 May 2017
This is what I think of your "resistance." It's an Astro-turfy toy of a sector of the ruling elite[.]

Michael Rectenwald @antipcnyuprof 15 May 2017
"Social justice" -- the worst misnomer of the 21st century, so far.

Michael Rectenwald @antipcnyuprof 7 May 2017
It's so tiring being morally condescended to by sententious virtue-signaling SJWs and PC police. I don't need them to tell me how to act.

Michael Rectenwald @antipcnyuprof 5 May 2017
I don't think I'd send another child of mine to college. I could teach them the chants myself: "No Trump, no KKK, No fascist USA!" etc.

Michael Rectenwald @antipcnyuprof 5 May 2017
Just watching as all the possible pleasures of human existence are being systematically destroyed by "social justice."

Michael Rectenwald @antipcnyuprof 26 Apr 2017
Gender studies, the new medieval scholasticism: Not how many angels can fit on the head of a pin but how many genders can fit on a spectrum.

APPENDIX B:
BEST FACEBOOK STATUSES

May 2, 2018
Leftists have actually achieved their Gramscian cultural hegemony --
and what a nightmare it is. Behold "social justice!"

 Michael Rectenwald
May 1 at 11:33pm · 🌐 ▾ ···

People need to stop cowing and quailing before the social justice mob. I'll
wear and say what I want.

'It's just a dress': Teen's Chinese prom attire stirs cultural appropriation debate

The Utah teenager was not expecting the wave of Twitter attacks in response to
her prom choice — a traditional Chinese dress known as a cheongsam or qipao.

WASHINGTONPOST.COM

👍 Like   💬 Comment   ↪ Share

 Derek Soulliere, Peter Y Paik and 64 others

3 Shares

25 Comments

April 30, 2018
Why don't we just rid ourselves of social identity entirely? The contemporary obsession with identity is a disabling and narcissistic waste of time, energy, and resources. Further, if identity categories are the basis of oppression, why the desire to cling to them?!

April 30, 2018
The next person who compares me to Jordan Peterson is fired.

April 22, 2018
Three major political forms prevailed over the last one hundred years: fascism, communism, and liberal democracy. Two out of the three are totalitarian. Take your pick. I know I have.

April 21, 2018
Leftists think that abstractions are real but others know that people and how they behave are much more real than abstractions. That's why leftists are shocked when a former leftist leaves their animal pack upon noticing what foul, vicious, rabid animals leftists are.

April 15, 2018
Circumstances are all-determining, except when they're not.

April 9, 2018
If I claim to be a king, can I get a kingdom prothesis?

April 5, 2018
Mass shooting has just improved its diversity, equity, and inclusion rating.

March 31, 2018
Every single population extant has been a colonizer and a conqueror at some point in history. In Joseph Conrad's Heart of Darkness, the first dark continent he refers to is Britain. It was colonized by the Romans. It is a colonizer by the time of the narration. That is, today's colonizers are yesterday's colonized and vice versa.

March 25, 2018
Today's Left is about as grassroots as an inflated hot-air balloon in a Macy's Day Parade.

March 25, 2018
The anti-gun high schooler corps (if they are all such) appears to be part of a mass-mediated attempt to rebrand an otherwise anti-SJW Gen Z so as to give them a burnished, pre-fab SJW gloss.

 Michael Rectenwald
March 25 · 🌐 ▼

Sounds quite familiar yet those lamenting the past cannot see its reproduction in their very midst.

China's Cultural Revolution: son's guilt over the mother he sent to her death

Zhang Hongbing was 16 when he denounced his mother for criticising Chairman Mao. Now Zhang wants to make amends

THEGUARDIAN.COM

👍 Like   💬 Comment   ↪ Share

Scott Ullman, Alexa Núñez and 18 others

7 Shares   2 Comments

March 24, 2018
Democrats want the world to end to prove Trump was as terrible as they've said.

March 24, 2018
The satiation of theoretical closure and the experience in the present of a utopia deferred. For some, these are joys in themselves.

March 23, 2018
Apples to apples and bananas to bananas—actually-existing capitalism must be compared to actually-existing socialism, not utopian idealist socialism.

March 16, 2018
Promote liberty over enforced values, esp. when those values abrogate liberty & otherwise have little to recommend them other than force itself.

March 16, 2018
Universities are perpetrating macro-aggressive totalitarianism as they police everyday parlance.

March 14, 2018
Some capitalists apparently promote Marxist socialism/communism/leftism/ - but only because rather than the abolition of capital, these historically and probably merely represent the consolidation of capital. "None Dare Call It Conspiracy" (1971), while sloppily written, was nevertheless essentially correct. Communism merely consolidates capital in the hands of an oligarchy. Whether this oligarchy consists of bureaucrats or capitalists matters little to the workers, although the former are worse to work for because they don't know what they are doing.

March 13, 2018
Today's Left is an agent of the state.

March 10, 2018
I am not advocating that anyone become a Nietzschean, btw. It's just that he is a good antidote for social-justice-type ressentiment ideologies.

March 10, 2018
"Social justice" ideology is an insidious social virus.

March 9, 2018
I've now read ten reviews of the Black Book of Communism in major academic journals and not one quibbles with the factual findings of the book. The only criticisms made are about the comparisons with the Holocaust, some quibbling about what the crimes mean in light of coterminous events, and whether all of the deaths by famine can be attributed to political desiderata. Also, none attempt to refute the findings that Lenin began the Red Terror with its mass political murders and concentration camps (the gulag came under Stalin). That's it. Not one refutes the figures: 96 million deaths.

March 7, 2018
Hey poll parrot and robotic chanting leftists: you're losing the actual war of the intellect. Your minds are so utterly flabby from disuse that it's almost unfair to ask you to express a thought.

March 7, 2018
Soon Twitter will have megaphone tweets for leftists to drown out those whose arguments they cannot defeat, just like on campuses.

March 7, 2018
Intersectionality, the playing field of the Oppression Olympics: On your mark...

March 7, 2018
The technology sector is controlled by leftist ideologues. They are driven by ideology and ideology trumps capital for these organizations -- unless, that is, they are being remunerated for supporting leftist ideology by some funding source, like George Soros, for example. In any case, they are purveying Maoist, Stalinist, and postmodernist politics.

One explanation for why major capitals are ostensibly supporting anti-capitalist ideologies is that anti-capitalism/socialism actually supports the consolidation of capital rather than, as advertised, its abolition.

March 6, 2018
North American higher education is a shit hole.

February 24, 2018
The contemporary LEFT has more in common with fascism than the contemporary right.

February 23, 2018
Nation busting is the new union busting.

February 28, 2018
Socialism is not a plan to overcome the ruling class and establish the collective ownership of the means of production. It is a plan to *consolidate* the ownership of the means of production in the hands of the oligarchy, with the masses as "equal."

February 17, 2018
I don't speak SJW.

February 16, 2018
They don't even understand Damore's argument, probably having never read it. These are phrase repeaters and poll parrots -- robotic, mindless drones, today's left.

February 12, 2018
A shameless will to power will be the inevitable response to all of the shackling and shaming of "privilege."

February 4, 2018
Every contact with Russia is now nefarious under the boogey man perspective. What does that make Bill and Hillary, as Bill received half a million dollars for speaking in Moscow right after the nuclear deal with Uranium One.

February 3, 2018
Mainstream media coddles the left, providing them a fact-free safe space where, immured from empirical reality, they can continue to germinate and gestate their delusions. It's truly frightening to observe.

February 3, 2018
Supporting spy agencies, vilifying Russia and cheering on the state to destroy US citizens is now called the "resistance." How far the left has fallen.

February 3, 2018
Today's left is INSANE, utterly INSANE. They live in a fact-free safe space.

February 3, 2018
The "Russian collusion" narrative is an empty, evidence-free smoke-screen, a deflection invented to protect and promote Hillary Clinton and to destroy Trump in case he won. The "resistance" is rooting for the deep state and their oligarchical overlords.

January 27, 2018
CNN wants to make cuckholds of us all. Soy channel.

January 27, 2018
The distinction I would draw is not between left and right but rather between libertarianism and authoritarianism/statism. Under this model, Antifa counts as part of the latter, not the former -- just for example. The Soros agenda of course is part of the latter, and this is why he funds activists who oppose the former.

January 18, 2018
The 1st Amendment does not protect all speech. It does not, for example, protect speech that leads to illegal activity and/or imminent violence, defamation, and libel. The 1st Amendment also does not protect speakers from liability for the foreseeable consequences of their speech.

I never claimed to be a free speech absolutist. And my "speech" amounted to criticism of an ideology and mechanisms prevalent in academia and beyond. I never once mentioned any individuals by name. I never once even engaged in ad hominem argumentation.

My attackers, however, showed no such restraint, and, in fact, they maliciously and mendaciously attacked me on public, official university email list servs with the explicit aim of damaging my professional reputation and endangering my career.

January 17, 2018
Real news is the news of a fake reality. Fake news is the news of real fakeness.

January 13, 2018
Dragon Slayer

In my dreams
I lead an army
Looking back
No one behind me
On the front line
My sword in hand
I slay the dragon
To save the land

Where is love
Why do I fight
Why am I lost
After I've won
Why is it night
After the dawn?

In my dreams
Criminality
Looking back
A herd behind me
My shadow hung
By a wet noose
On paid leave
But I can't get loose

Where is love
Why do I fight
Why am I lost
After I've won
Why is it night
After the dawn?

In my dreams
I lead a real life
Looking back
She's in plain sight
I'll be damned

If I do and
If I don't
Give up hope

Where is love
Why do I fight
Why am I lost
After I've won
Why is it night
After the dawn?

January 9, 2018
To "identify as" is to suggest that one is really two entities at once. "'I' identify as 'X'" means "I" and "X" are not one but rather two entities held together by a conjunctive verb construction. Thus the schizoid personalities of the "social justice" era.

January 3, 2018
Not even God has been thought able to judge people in groups. Social justice is impossible, a contradiction. This is to say nothing for the moment of the fact that it is a complete misnomer, that "social justice" involves nothing like justice in any true sense. Social justice is a postmodernist appropriation of Stalinist and Maoist ideological purging, indoctrination and conformity-imposing mechanisms. It's often brutal, vicious and cruel. No justice to see here folks. Move along.

January 1, 2018
Liberalism
1. Freedom: defend freedom of speech/thought.
2. Equality: defend legal equality of individuals, not special privileges for special identity groups.
3. Authoritarianism: reject state/social authoritarianism, mobbing & witch hunts.

December 29, 2017
Professor "All I want for Christmas Is White Genocide" George Ciccariello-Maher has resigned from Drexel, blaming the rightwing and comparing himself to Franz Fanon. LOL. The height of paranoid delusion, arrogance, and grandiosity.

December 13, 2017
The oligarchy is behind identity politics.

December 12, 2017
Moral outrage is the contemporary (il)liberal's favorite pastime.

December 11, 2017
The Democrats are the new religious fundamentalists. Their religion is "social justice" ideology.

December 11, 2017
There are no classes. There are no species. There are no varieties. There are only individuals.

December 2, 2017
Gender is not a social construction. The social construction is the idea that gender is a social construction.

Addendum: I do know very well the "difference" between "gender" and "sex." I happen to have a Ph.D. in Theory. While I do believe that gender itself as such is socially mediated and involves socialization processes and social expectations, I do not believe, as the current orthodoxy would have it, that SEX difference does not exist in human beings. That's right; that is the current orthodoxy. It derives from transgender theory and is sheer lunacy.

November 28, 2017
The "micro-aggression" finders will soon find their safe spaces implode when their own aggressions and totalitarianism are exposed. Stay tuned.

November 16, 2017
Answer to an NYU survey question:

We are interested in knowing more about your experiences. If you would like to elaborate on why you seriously considered leaving, please do so here.

I have found that my program and colleagues are ideologically bigoted, anti-intellectual, opposed to diversity of thought, hostile to differing views, defamatory to those with whom they disagree, uncivil, puerile, vicious, mendacious, close-minded, censorious, cultish, herd-like, group-thinking, indoctrinated, intolerant, zealously self-righteous, and deflecting. They accuse one of racism, sexism, and bullying even as they are the only ones engaging in said activities. NYU has fostered the most essentialist, constraining and superficial notions of "diversity," an utterly limited and limiting understanding that ends up tokenizing those with the exterior markers of superficial "difference," while utterly missing the entire point of anti-discrimination -- that people should not be evaluated on the basis of their appearance or other identity markers.

November 15, 2017
I just got lectured by Siri for inappropriate language. I used a certain word. And Siri chided me, saying: "Michael, your language!" At which point I swore at her again, and she shut down and would not respond. I'm now being dictated to by a Social Justice Robot.

November 14, 2017
It's official: I am a cultural and social libertarian.

November 6, 2017
I don't require that my friends pass ideological litmus tests or recite shibboleths & slogans. If anything, I demand that they don't. I demand that they think.

October 27, 2017
Sesame cold noodles, deviled eggs. Let's see, what else is best served cold? I love cold dishes.

October 25, 2017
Trump: urination, maybe.
Clinton: uranium, definitely.

October 14, 2017
Marx(ism): first as tragedy, then as farce.

October 11, 2017
Already a year ago, but soon a book.

September 28, 2017
"We find it of course ironic that figures such as Rectenwald still receive a salary by 'progressive' institutions, yet those who speak out against white supremacists, bigotry and fascism are punished," the group said over Facebook messenger.

What is "ironic" about a "progressive" institution having anti-authoritarian/anti-totalitarian professor? Also, you do know that Isaacson's tweets fantasize about cutting his students' throats after they become cops in a confrontation with Antifa. He also called for the assassination of Trump and Pence ("assassinate Pence first," he advised). That is actually a felony offense. And you defend this clearly unhinged lunatic?

As an admitted advocate of cop-killing, do you really believe he should be trusted to teach students training to be police officers?

One more thing: No committee for "Diversity, Equity and Inclusion" (Conformity, Inequity and Exclusion) at John Jay has condemned him for his heinous statements, yet I was denounced by an *official* NYU Liberal Studies committee for criticizing an ideology and its mechanisms, a perfectly reasonable and utterly unassailable exercise of academic freedom. I said nothing about or against any groups (other than SJWs), "races," gender identities, or people of various sexual orientations. I critiqued an ideology and its official adoption by the university. Yet I was denounced within 48 hours and put on leave. Now tell me about "irony" and double standards. You just expect everyone to buy into your ideology and that those who don't do not deserve to teach or even to live, likely. Who's the totalitarian here? Surely not I.

September 23, 2017
If the problem is the loss of self-determination, indoctrination into idiocy and self-satisfied consumption, the ideologies that ensure one-dimensionality, flattening of life to satisfaction of needs, the invention of new ones, and their satisfaction, ad infinitum -- then the answer is not Marcuse's social one, but Charles Bukowski.

September 14, 2017
Pumpkin Spice Latte now "racist" according to lunatic SJW left: http://www.legitgov.org/Pumpkin-Spice-Lattes-fund-white-supremacy-Trump-White-House-feminist-group

September 13, 2017
Red-pilling isn't the right-wing-ing of a person but their unlocking from left self-righteousness and ideologically-blinkered obeisance to authoritarianism. It's freedom from the matrix of mass indoctrination.

September 10, 2017
Here are the results of Facebook responses to every gender cue I could construe in the gender field in the profile "basics" section. Notice that "man" and "woman" are not options.

September 7, 2017
Somehow banishment from the herd suits me.

September 6, 2017
I got a new office, a "safe space" in a bldg. away from SJW mob & Antifa faculty dreck. **SJWs create a need for that which they demand.**

August 31, 2017
It's so fun being spied on while having counterintelpro telling you exactly what they are looking at and for.

August 29, 2017
SJWs want to destroy everything beautiful, powerful and brilliant. Theirs is a ressentiment ideology and a subtractive egalitarianism, a leveling ideology that seeks to thwart and crush anything approaching greatness, because they have none in them, at all, and never will. They are the equivalent of pieces of broken, circular AI software running indefinitely. The AI agent system constructs syntagms from pre-fabricated units of phrasing found on the web. The syntagms never produce new meaning. SJWs do not have what we call "thoughts."

August 24, 2017
The educational system in North America is a giant SJW sausage factory.

August 19, 2017
Trumpism represents the scraps of identity politics that the Democrats left for dead.

August 14, 2017
The postmodernist is like a person attempting to milk a tree. When asked why he is trying to milk a tree, he responds that the word "tree" is an arbitrary designation and bears no necessary correspondence with the object designated as such. The word to designate what we call a "tree" could very well have been the word "cow." Thus, he proceeds to milk the tree, I mean "cow."

August 10, 2017
The weakest arguments are the ones most likely to require authoritarianism to impose compliance by force. This happened in the Soviet Union with its anti-science (Lysenkoism) and it is happening in the west with its new anti-science: (trans)gender theory.

August 9, 2017
Contemporary gender theory = contemporary Lysenkoism.

July 18, 2017
Postmodernism is not simply some bizarre fascination of the lunatic Left. It is now actually *the* dominant ideology of the time, which means that we live in a postmodern era. The notion that everything, including science, is a closed linguistic system without especial reference to any corresponding reality; that all "truths" are merely narratives; that each group and/or "self" has their own special standpoint epistemology and their own "truth," which can neither be falsified nor verified by anyone else; that bodies, genders, "sexual differences" and the rest of the nonsense of which "selves" (and everyone has many "selves") consist are merely social constructs from which the world is made as if from so much linguistic and ideational silly putty -- this is now the mainstream Weltanschauung of the era.

June 14, 2017
Leftists have been symbolically beheading and murdering Trump for weeks now, with no chastisement from their leadership. It's no wonder one of their foot soldiers understood such silence as an an endorsement for the real thing. He couldn't get to Trump so he found a few proxies and opened fire.

June 10, 2017
Soon, the humanities, the social sciences, and maybe even the sciences will amount to people walking around holding mirrors that reflect their identities. The only credential that will count in academia will be one's identity, period. Basically, the humanities are amounting to nothing more than ever-multiplying niche markets of narcissism posing as radicalism. It does not at all matter what you know, nor even who you know really, but rather, exclusively WHAT you ARE, from an identity standpoint. Academia is becoming an utter sham.

June 3, 2017
I'm convinced that the Left will never again be (if it ever even was)
a world-historical force. The Left-Right divide is a faux construction
to disable the real confrontation -- the confrontation between the
bottom and the top.

June 2, 2017
So [Kathy] Griffin simulated a Trump beheading and now complains of
Trump family "bullying?" Remember everything an SJW accuses you of
doing to them is exactly what they are doing to you.

May 19, 2017
The primary characteristic of totalitarian ideologues is essentially
moral arrogance, a complete lack of moral humility, and the certain
conviction that they themselves are justice incarnate. They thus believe that they are completely justified to exert their will to achieve
their desired ends "by any means necessary." Such ideologues rejoiced
when God was declared "dead," as such, because now they could
assume the authority of God for themselves.

May 18, 2017
Art should not be run through ideological councils or committees for
approval or banishment.

May 17, 2017

Fantastic! We at Stanford University are delighted to have such an innovative, articulate and verbally talented student such as yourself.

Given the content of your essay, we have also decided to grant you a full scholarship, inclusive of tuition and room and board. We do expect you to attend any events where right-leaning speakers are able to reach the lectern, and to similarly repeat phrases without end, just as you have here in your excellent admissions essay.

Your education at Stanford will consist exclusively of the inculcation of the very ideology that you have so wonderfully displayed in your statement of purpose essay. Essentially, think of Stanford as a Social Justice Warrior incubator; our mission is to produce students who will repeat phrases endlessly, refuse to listen to differing perspectives, and finally, to serve as carriers of this ideology to the wider culture. We are confident that you are just such a candidate. Congratulations!

Sincerely,

SJW Officer of Admissions,
Stanford University

May 17, 2017
I don't care what gender(s) or non-gender(s) people claim for themselves. That is entirely their prerogative and I have no objection to anyone's gender identification, whatever it may or may not be. I will accede to their self-identification, including a relatively reasonable pronoun semantics.

But don't try to make me subscribe to the notion and declare it true that sexual difference does not exist in human beings. This claim is ... a matter of anti-empirical religiosity, and I will not pretend that it's true. Take me to the gulag if it comes down to that. But sexual difference does exist in human beings and without sexual difference human beings could not reproduce -- unless, that is, we turned into asexual organisms, which is a great unlikelihood.

May 16, 2017
One thing I am pointing out in my book is that today's social justice movement does not have its roots in religious social justice movements such as Tikkun or the Catholic worker. Or even the Civil Rights movement. The roots are in left totalitarianisms.

May 16, 2017
The shaming techniques that the Left engages in -- callout culture, self-criticism, privilege checking, etc. -- all have Maoism as their provenance.

May 15, 2017
I've just received an email from Hillary Clinton, replete with a new logo (below) for what appears to be an attempt at political resuscitation. I hit the unsubscribe button and gave this reason in the allotted space:

Are you out of your mind, you deep-state conspirator and globalist fraud? You should have the dignity to quietly leave public life and leave the future in other hands than yours (or other Clintons for that matter). You are nothing but a neocon in Democratic clothing. Your party's complicity in deep-state, neocon objectives is glaringly obvious, even in the "resistance" to Trump, who's already acceded to the game plan.

You're fooling no one with this pathetic attempt to re-enter the fray. Go away!

Michael Rectenwald
Professor, NYU

May 14, 2017
To what extent is the CIA involved in producing and exacerbating the increasing fractiousness of the U.S. Left? Before you cry "conspiracy," consider this: they did fund feminism (Gloria Steinem), abstract expressionism, and the Iowa Writing Workshop. Why not fund SJWs?

May 12, 2017
Strange how readers read an essay criticizing SJW ideology and then bitterly complain that the author has not abided by SJW ideology, and thus is culpable in the reader's mind for some offense against the precious (and totalitarian) creed.

May 9, 2017
The histrionics about Trump's "authoritarian" takeover are afoot again. But no one can seem to make clear what the indications of this are. Firing Comey, who was just accused of exaggerating CLINTON's malfeasance? Tanks rolling down the streets? Just what?

Meanwhile, the worst authoritarians I see today are on the left -- the Antifa, the SJWs, and everyone else shutting down speech and enforcing their codes of anti-liberty.

May 9, 2017
SJWs operate in pack and attack mobs. If you seek asylum from their baseless slander, libel, and defamation of character, they call you a "snowflake," imagining that they proffer a clever reversal. The problem is, and I've said this many times, SJWs create a need for that which they demand by virtue of their culture of grievance and dog-piling. Eventually, they almost all become victims of their own tactics, as SJW ideology is a self-immolating creed of one-downsmanshp, a competition for who's the ultimate victim. Victimology produces real victims.

May 5, 2017
If someone I know claims to be a dog, I am not letting them sit at the dining room table any longer. They will eat out of a bowl on the floor.

April 30, 2017
I'm documenting all the craziness for future generations, in case there are any.

April 28, 2017
I think there are Leftbook groups who send people to my wall to antagonize me, and that attacking me has some status-signifying value somewhere. One after another they come, like suicide bombers. (After all, they all become dead to me when I block them.)

April 26, 2017
Playing the victim cloaks a surreptitious will to power.

April 21, 2017
If we allow activists to be the arbiters of allowable speech, sooner or later the Overton window of allowable speech will close on their own necks.

April 20, 2017
People don't often say what they think but rather what they think is permissible.

April 13, 2017
I see many have their outrage generators running at full or near-full capacity tonight.

April 11, 2017
Leftism's most conspicuous falsity is the will to power veiled in the disguise of other-interest. It's for the workers. It's for the poor. It's for the subaltern. It's for the marginalized. But aren't all these mere fodder for the leftist's self-assertion and power plays? Naked will to power is much more respectable and true. Safety pins be damned.

April 7, 2017
Trump warned by deep-state neocon Repubs & Dems--do regime change in Syria & elsewhere or "collusion w/Russia" story ruins your presidency.

April 5, 2017
The university is being utterly destroyed by PC authoritarianism, SJW ideology and identity politics.

April 3, 2017
Someone just told me, "No one takes your bullshit seriously." My answer was, "No one has even heard of your bullshit, so there."

April 3, 2017
No amount of evidence or logical argument will make SJWs and fellow travelers recognize that they either implicitly or explicitly endorse authoritarianism -- that they are essentially wannabe totalitarians.

April 2, 2017
Twitter is not a social media outlet, it is *social justice* media outlet. Author of six books, full professor at NYU, TV pundit, and recognized spokesman for campus free speech, I am still not "official" on Twitter. Yet liberals & leftists without a shred of real accomplishments are made official simply for regurgitating the right social justice pabulum.

April 1, 2017
Funny how many experts on academia haven't set foot on a campus in 10-20 years.

March 29, 2017
"Social justice" is a ruling ideology & social justice activists are a neo-liberal police force.

APPENDIX C:
SELECTED MEDIA COVERAGE, ESSAYS, TALKS, AND INTERVIEWS

SELECTED MEDIA COVERAGE

"Kanye Broke Progressivism with Seven Words." *The Independent Whig*. 24 April 2018.

"Towards a Cognitive Theory of Politics." *Quillette*. 20 April 2018.

"Tribalism, Reason, and the Challenges Raised by Global Neoliberal Capitalism." *Dissident Voice*. 7 April 2018.

"Finding Our Own Free Voices." *Martha Cohen Blog. The Times of Israel.* 30 March 2018.

"Now Inclusion Means Exclusion." *National Review*. 14 March 2018.

"Ex-Communist Professor Sues NYU." *Confessions of a College Professor*. 1 March 2018.

"Halt the march of liberal fascism." *The Gainesville Sun*. 16 February 2018.

"National Association of Scholars Holds Event on Academic Freedom." *Washington Square News*. 6 February 2018.

"'Deplorable' NYU prof slaps colleagues with lawsuit." *Campus Reform*. 31 January 2018.

"'All Hell Broke Loose': NYU Prof Suing School After Being 'Coerced' Into Paid Leave for Criticizing PC Culture." *Fox News Insider*. 29 January 2018.

"'Deplorable' Prof Sues NYU.' Campus Unmasked. *Rebel Media*. 29 January 2018

"'Deplorable' NYU Professor Sues University, Colleagues for Defamation." *Washington Square News*. 29 January 2018.

"The White Man's Tale." *The Atheist Conservative*. 28 January 2018.

"Meet the Anti-PC Professor." *Education Watch International*. 28 January 2018.

"Why Political Correctness Is Incorrect." *International Business Times*. 25 January 2018.

"'Anti-PC' Professor Michael Rectenwald is Suing NYU and Four Professors For Defamation and Wants You to Know It." *NYU Local*. 24 January 2018.

"Professor: I was 'ambushed' by progressives for criticizing campus PC culture." *The College Fix*. 22 January 2018.

"'Deplorable' Professor Fights Back Against Campus Totalitarians: An interview with the 'Anti-PC NYU Prof.'" *FrontPage Magazine*. 22 January 2018.

"Politically Incorrect NYU Professor Sues Colleagues for Defamation." *Accuracy in Academia*. 18 January 2018.

"The Hypocrisy of Political Correctness." *AMAC*. 18 January 2018.

"NYU Prof Files Suit After Being Ousted for 'Non-PC' Speech." *The Jewish Voice*. 17 January 2018.

"Anti-PC Professor sues NYU for defamation." *iOTW REPORT.com*. 16 January 2018.

"Paybacks Are Annoying, NYU Finds." *Accuracy in Academia*. 16 January 2018.

"EXCLUSIVE: Anti-PC Professor Suing NYU Speaks Out." *The Daily Caller*. 15 January 2018.

"'Deplorable' NYU prof sues university, colleagues for defamation." *Fox News*. 14 January 2018.

"'Deplorable' NYU professor sues colleagues for defamation." *New York Post*. 13 January 2018.

"Halloween: US universities warn students against culturally insensitive costumes." *Independent*. 31 October 2017.

"NYU's Deplorable Professor Goes After John Jay Professor Over 'Dead Cops.'" *Washington Square News*. 27 September 2017.

"NYU Professor calls on John Jay College President to terminate Mike Isaacson." *Far Left Watch*. 7 September 2017.

"'Deplorable NYU Professor' Slams Peers' Embrace of Antifa Violence." *Lifezette/ Polizette*. 23 August 2017.

"NYU Prof: Many Leftists Are 'Wannabe Totalitarians.'" *Daily Wire*. 23 August 2017.

"The Monster Hiding Under Our Beds Isn't Trump; It's the Media." *Downtrend.com*. 23 August 2017.

"Political Incorrectness is Treated More Harshly Than Actual Hate Speech. Why?" *Intellectual Takeout*. 10 August 2017.

"The Left's Factions Increasingly Turning Their Sights on Each Other." *Townhall*. 3 July 2017.

"The Unhinged Left." *Intellectual Conservative*. 21 June 2017.

"Leodora: The world of political correctness isn't perfect." *The Times Herald*. 3 April 2017.

"'Disappearing' the Scholar/Author (Updated)." *Academe Blog*. 31 March 2017.

"The Opioid Epidemic Is This Generation's AIDS Crisis." *New York Magazine*. 16 March 2017.

"Professor: Leftist-driven refugee, immigration policies 'existential threat to the US.'" *The College Fix*. 6 March 2017.

"Anti-PC Prof: Michael Rectenwald." *WNYU Radio*. March 2017.

"Michael Rectenwald, doing a Christopher Hitchens?" *Libcom*. 28 February 2017.

"Sick! Slate posts VENOMOUS piece on Alan Colmes after he dies, railing him because he worked for Fox." *Bizpac Review*. 24 February 2017.

"Lib NYU prof's DONE with 'obscene, abusive, fanatical' people on the intolerant Left after feeling their wrath." *BizPac Review*. 23 February 2017.

"NYU Professor and Former Leftist: Nothing Comes Close to Personal Invective, Insults, and Degrading Imagery of the Left." *The Gateway Pundit*. 22 February 2017.

"New Anti-PC Novel 'My Safe Space' Satirizes Overreaction to Trump." *HeatStreet*. 9 February 2017.

"Professor Says SJW Platform Undermines Free Speech." *One America News Network*. 6 February 2017.

"Reply to LS Diversity, Equity and Inclusion Working Group." *Washington Square News*. 6 February 2017.

"Protests and Attacks Cut Gavin McInnes's Speech Short." *Washington Square News*. 2 February 2017.

"Twitter removes post by NYU professor who blasted PC culture on college campuses." *Fox News.* 24 January 2017.

"Twitter removed my 'SJW ideology' post with no explanation, says anti-PC professor." *The College Fix.* 23 January 2017.

"Challenging A Professor's Anti-White Tweets Isn't Censorship." *The Daily Caller.* 26 December 2016.

"The West's Politically Correct Dictatorship: It Has Blinded Us to the Real Danger: Radical Islam." *Gatestone Institute International Policy Council.* 6 December 2016.

"NYU releases vocal Anti-PC Professor on paid leave." *Pace Press.* 5 December 2016.

"A living glossary of all the words you need to understand the Trump presidency." *Quartz.* 29 November 2016.

"Did NYU Do Right by Michael Rectenwald?." *Odyssey.* 21 November 2016.

"Anti-PC NYU Professor Is Now Promoted." *Washington Square News.* 18 November 2016.

"NYU Promotes 'Deplorable' Professor." *Inside Higher Ed.* 15 November 2016.

"NYU strikes a blow for diversity of thought." *New York Post.* 14 November 2016.

"NYU Professor on Leave for 'Anti-PC' Views Is Reinstated, Awarded Promotion." *The Daily Caller.* 14 November 2016.

"NYU brings back professor who blasted PC culture, gives him a raise." *Fox News.* 14 November 2016.

"NYU Brings Back 'Deplorable Professor,' Awards Him a Raise." *Heat Street.* 13 November 2016.

"'Deplorable' NYU professor gets a promotion." *New York Post.* 13 November 2016.

"'Deplorable NYU Professor' on PC culture." *Varney and Company,* Fox Business News. 11 November 2016.

"Campus PC culture - So rampant that NYU is paying to silence me." *St. Paul Pioneer Press.* 10 November 2017.

"The Real Villains of Higher Education." *Pacific Standard.* 10 November 2016.

"The End of Academic Freedom?" *The NCC Advocacy Chapter (NAAC) of the American Association of University Professors (AAUP).* 7 November 2016

"Anti-PC Professor in High Demand." *Washington Square News.* 7 November 2016.

"NYU Challenges 'Deplorable' Professor's Claims." *Inside Higher Ed.* 7 November 2016.

"Michael Rectenwald Wants to Make the American Left Great Again." *NYU Local.* 6 November 2016.

"NYU professor on leave after blasting PC culture fires back." *Fox News.* 6 November 2016.

"The Ivory Tower's Troikas." *Death Metal Underground.* 5 November 2016.

"NYU professor suspended after anti-PC comments." *Kentucky Kernel.* 5 November 2016.

"Despite Inconsistent Stories, Anti-PC Prof Should Return to Classes." *Washington Square News.* 4 November 2016.

"University Gives Anti PC Professor Ultimatum on Paid Leave." *Washington Square News.* 4 November 2016.

"Professor 'fired after mocking political correctness' story falls apart." *Boing Boing.* 4 November 2016.

"Michael Rectenwald the 'Deplorable NYU Professor': I'm Not a Fake!." *Heat Street.* 4 November 2016.

"Did 'Deplorable' Prof Unmask Extreme PC Culture at NYU?." *Minding the Campus.* 4 November 2016.

"NYU's Mysterious, Anti-P.C. "Deplorable" Prof Has Been Unveiled." *Slate.* 4 November 2016.

"A Communist NYU Professor Says He Was Ousted for Mocking Political Correctness. Was He?." *Daily Intelligencer, New York Magazine.* 3 November 2016.

"Rigged Polls: Tests Show College Grads Conceal Support For Donald Trump." *Breitbart News.* 3 November 2016.

"Here's what happened when I challenged the PC campus culture at NYU." *The Washington Post.* 3 November 2016.

"NYU professor says he was encouraged to go on leave because of his tweeting and his newspaper interview." *Washington Post.* 3 November 2016.

"Cast Out for Criticizing PC: The 21st-Century Inquisition: The punishment of NYU's Michael Rectenwald should worry us all." *Spiked.* 2 November 2016.

"NYU Welcoming Back Deplorable Professor." *The Daily Caller.* 2 November 2016.

"New York University Professor on Paid Leave After Criticizing Trigger Warnings and Safe Spaces." *University Herald.* 2 November 2016.

"The Strange Saga of 'Deplorable NYU Prof'." *Adweek.* 1 November 2016.

"Prof Takes Stand Against Political Correctness; PC Gestapo Reacts INSTANTLY." The Federalist Papers. 1 November 2016.

"NYU Professor Criticized Trigger Warnings. Now He's on Leave for the Semester." Reason. 1 November 2016.

"NYU Says Leave Was Voluntary for Professor Who Criticized Political Correctness. The Chronicle of Higher Education. 1 November 2016.

"'Deplorable' NYU Prof on Leave." Inside Higher Ed. 1 November 2016.

"Welcome to the Latest Culture Wars." CounterPunch. 31 October 2016.

"Professor who tweeted against PC culture booted from New York University." News.com.au. 31 October 2016.

"Anti-SJW Professor Forced Out at New York University." Breitbart News. 31 October 2016.

"NYU professor who tweeted against 'safe space' campus culture placed on leave." The Washington Times. 31 October 2016.

"At NYU, watch out if you're railing against PC insanity." New York Post. 31 October 2016.

"Michael Rectenwald: NYU Prof, Victim of PC Gestapo." This Ain't Hell. 31 October 2016.

"Anti-PC professor goes on leave after 'Inclusion Working Group' complains about him." *The College Fix*. 31 October 2017.

"@DeplorableNYUProf [@antipcnyuprof] Ousted from New York University After Criticizing PC Culture." *HeatStreet.* 31 October 2016.

"NYU Prof Ousted For Anti-PC Twitter Campaign." *The Daily Caller*. 30 October 2016.

"NYU Places 'Deplorable NYU' Professor on Paid Leave." *NYU Local.* 30 October 2016.

"Professor who tweeted against PC culture is out at NYU." *New York Post.* 30 October 2016.

"Elite College Professor Calls Academia a Mad House and 'Safe Spaces' an Existential Error." *HeatStreet.* 27 October 2016.

"NYU Professor Created Undercover Twitter Account to Blast 'Safe Space' College Culture." *Fox News.* 26 October 2016.

"NYU professor who posed as alt-right Twitter user is found 'guilty of illogic and incivility'." *The Washington Times.* 26 October 2016.

"NYU professor created undercover Twitter account to blast 'safe space' college culture." *The Washington Times.* 25 October 2016.

Letter to the Editor: Liberal Studies Rejects @antipcnyuprof's Faulty Claims. *Washington Square News.* 25 October 2016.

"NYU prof attacks 'viral identity politics of academia.'" *Campus Reform.* 24 October 2016.

"The Trump Treatment for a Campus Conservative." *Accuracy in Academia.* 20 October 2016.

"Three Books, One Year." *Carnegie Mellon University.* 28 September 2015.

SELECTED RELEVANT ESSAYS AND PRESENTATIONS

"Introduction to 'Social Justice.'" New York Metropolitan Republican Club. 3 May 2018.

"'Social Justice' and Its Postmodern Parentage." *Academic Questions.* 31.2. 10 April 2018. 1-10.

"Why Political Correctness Is Incorrect." *International Business Times.* 25 January 2018.

"Shaming & Shunning, Part II: 'You Must Be a Rightwing Nut-job.'" *CLG News.* 30 August. 2017.

"Shaming & Shunning: The People Who Do It, & Its Likely Effects (Part I)." *CLG News* 16 August. 2017.

"A Critique of 'Social Justice' Ideology: Thinking through Marx and Nietzsche." *CLG News.* 20 July 2017.

"A Sketch Toward a Genealogy of 'Social Justice' Morals" (Part of The New Thought Police - Social Justice Warriors) YouTube. 3 June 2017.

"'Have You Found That Place That Makes You Want to Swallow Its Rhetoric Whole?'" *Quillette.* 6 May 2017.

"(Re)Secularizing the University." *American Conservative.* 14 March 2017.

"Reply to LS Diversity, Equity and Inclusion Working Group." *Washington Square News.* 6 February 2017.

"The Inauguration of Trump and the Early Opposition to Trumpism." *CLG News.* 23 January 2017.

"Here's what happened when I challenged the PC campus culture at NYU." *The Washington Post.* 3 November 2016.

"Trigger Warnings, Safe Spaces, Bias Reporting: The New Micro-techniques of Surveillance and Control." *CLG News.* 12 September 2016.

"From the Vampire Castle to Duck Dynasty: The Ideals of Identity Politics and How it Functions." *The North Star.* 22 December 2013.

"What's Wrong With Identity Politics (and Intersectionality Theory)? A Response to Mark Fisher's "Exiting the Vampire Castle" (And Its Critics)." *The North Star.* 2 December 2013.

"Postmodernism, the Academic Left, and the Crisis of Capitalism." *Insurgent Notes*. 11 March 2013.

SELECTED INTERVIEWS

Springtime for Snowflakes: Dr. Michael Rectenwald Interview." *The Liberalist*. 4 April 2018.

"The Ugly Truth About Social Justice | Michael Rectenwald and Stefan Molyneux." *FreedomRadio.com*. 17 February 2018.

"THE MILO SHOW 02/12/18: 'Deplorable NYU Professor' Michael Rectenwald." *Dangerous.com*. 12 February 2018. "Original Sin" (podcast version).

"Fighting the SJW Left with Professor Michael Rectenwald." *The Liberalist*. 2 February 2018.

"'Deplorable' professor sues New York University after his colleagues compared him to Satan and said he was thinking the wrong thoughts." *Tucker Carlson Tonight*. Fox News. 29 January 2018.

"'Deplorable' Professor Fights Back Against Campus Totalitarians: An interview with the 'Anti-PC NYU Prof.'" *FrontPage Magazine*. 22 January 2018.

"'Deplorable' NYU professor suing for defamation." *MSN*. 16 January 2018.

"'Deplorable' NYU professor suing for defamation." *Fox & Friends*. Fox News. 16 January 2018.

"Jordan Peterson, Michael Rectenwald (@antipcnyuprof), & John Kirbow Counter 'Social Justice.'" YouTube. 2 July 2017.

"Is political correctness harming the nation?." *The O'Reilly Factor*. 28 March 2017.

"A 'Deplorable' Professor on Why Campuses Are Reactionary and Anti-Intellectual." *The Contributing Factor,* Fox News. 20 February 2017.

"NYU Professor: Leftist 'Social Justice Warriors' Hinder Equality." *One America News Network.* 7 February 2017.

"A Conversation with NYU's 'Deplorable Professor.'" *NYU Politics Society Podcast.*.

"'Deplorable NYU Professor' on PC culture." *Varney and Company,* Fox Business News. 11 November 2016.

"Deplorable NYU Professor Wins Victory Over SJWs." *The Tom Woods Show.* 21 December 2016.

"My Chat with 'DeplorableNYUProf.' Michael Rectenwald (THE SAAD TRUTH_301)." *Gad Saad.* 5 December 2016.

"The Interview: Michael Rectenwald - NYU Professor." *Independent Man.* 1 December 2016.

"Michael Rectenwald on 'Trigger `Warnings' and the Origin of the Alt Right." *Maverick Philosopher.* 3 November 2016.

"Michael Rectenwald Interview." The MalaCast.

"Q&A With a Deplorable NYU Professor." *Washington Square News.* 24 October 2016.

CPSIA information can be obtained
at www.ICGtesting.com
Printed in the USA
LVHW092254280319
612278LV00001B/259/P